MEDIA

Marek Mularczyk

Transform Your World

— with —

Adobe
Photoshop
CS6/CC

Transform Your World with Adobe Photoshop CS6/CC

Published by M2 Media.

ISBN - 978-0-9571214-7-8 (Paperback)
ISBN - 978-0-9571214-8-5 (Digital Version)

www.marekmularczyk.com
Cover Design: Marek Mularczyk and Ernesto Lozada-Uzuriaga

Contents

Lesson 04
Image Retouching   113

Lesson 12
Adobe Camera Raw 359

Introduction

When I started using Adobe Photoshop (back in version 7), it was a bit simpler application (at that time it still shipped as Adobe Photoshop and Adobe ImageReady, does anyone remember that?). As Photoshop is evolving and getting more and more tools, it gets slightly more complicated and this is something I often hear from users new to Photoshop on my courses. They say it looks so complicated. My goal here will be to guide you through the "Photoshop world" step-by-step and make it easy-to-understand for you.

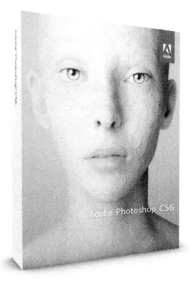

Adobe Photoshop is a default choice for digital imaging with its strong performance and powerful features for image editing. At the same time it offers a very intuitive interface. With Photoshop CS6, Adobe Camera Raw is included - a powerful plug-in used for editing or one could say "developing" raw images (and nowadays JPEGs and TIFFs as well).

Each new version of Photoshop pushes the boundaries of what is possible in digital imaging world and this book will try to explain it to you in an easy to understand language, step-by-step, without lots of jargon.

If you have used Photoshop before, you can skip some lessons and jump straight into the lessons you are interested in. If you are new to Photoshop, I encourage you to follow the lessons in order starting from Lesson 1. The way the book is structured, each new lesson builds on what you have learnt in previous lessons as well as it introduces new concepts and new techniques.

Before you start

Before you start, here's what you need to know:

- this book doesn't require any knowledge of Photoshop

- it does require some knowledge of your operating system, you need to know how to use your computer

- Photoshop works in the same way on both Windows and Mac computers, so you can use it interchangeably on both platforms

Installing Photoshop CS6

Before you start, you need to install Photoshop CS6. x, Adobe announced availability of the next version of Photoshop - Photoshop CC. Let me explain how to install Photoshop CS6 first and then I'll explain how to install Photoshop CC.

By the time you're reading this book, Photoshop CC will become available so you won't be able to purchase Photoshop CS6 from Adobe website any more. Because of that, I will assume that if you are using Photoshop CS6, you have purchased it earlier and you have it already installed or you purchased it as a download or as a boxed product and you're ready to install it.

If you have Photoshop ready to install it, just put the disc into your dvd drive (if you purchased boxed version of Photoshop CS6) and follow the steps for installation. If you purchased Photoshop as a download, extract the files and follow the steps to install it on your computer.

If you are using Photoshop CS6, you may be using either a standard version of Photoshop CS6 or Photoshop CS6 Extended (more on differences between them later in this chapter):

NEW Adobe Photoshop CS6 Extended Get all the imaging   NEW Adobe Photoshop CS6 Get state-of-the-art imaging magic.

Photoshop CS6 comes as a stand-alone application as well as part of Creative Suite and Creative Cloud, so can be purchased with all Creative Suite editions and Creative Cloud (as shown on the screenshot here):

Installing Photoshop CC

Installing Photoshop CC is slightly different from installing Photoshop CS6 as Photoshop CC is only available through Creative Cloud.

To install Photoshop CC (you can install it on a trial basis as well), you could:

* go to *https://www.adobe.com/uk/products/photoshop.html* and click **Log in to Creative Cloud** on the right side of the page:

- or you could go straight to Creative Cloud page using this link: *https://creative.adobe.com/*:

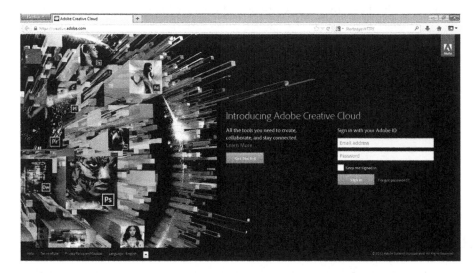

Once you're on Creative Cloud page, you log in to your account (or create an account if you don't have it, you can use your existing Adobe ID).

Once you've logged in, you will see your Creative Cloud page with all applications listed (you may need to click **Apps** in the top left corner):

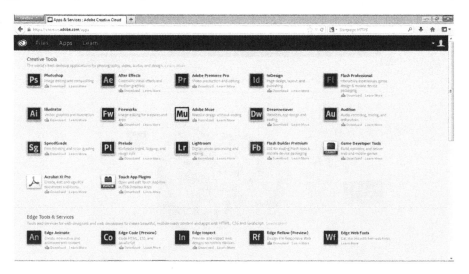

Now you can click **Download** under **Photoshop** to start download and installation of Photoshop on your computer:

Just follow the steps to install it and you'll be ready to go.

Adobe Photoshop CS6 Extended

Adobe Photoshop CS6 Extended includes some additional features that are not available in Standard edition. The features include:

*   Importing 3D images and editing them by painting, cloning, and retouching them.

*   Support for 3D files such as: U3D, Collada, KMZ, OBJ, and 3DS.

*   Support for file formats such as DICOM for medical scans, and MATLAB for developing algorithms.

Working with the lessons

This book comes with exercise files so that you can follow along to make the learning process easier.

The files can be downloaded by following the link below:

http://bit.ly/16hsjfG

Download the files, extract them and copy them onto your computer to your preferred location. During the exercises I'm going to keep the files on my desktop as an example. If you prefer use your own images. Not all the files are included in download as some images come from online libraries and I will be giving you the link where you could download or purchase them.

Keep Photoshop updated (Photoshop CS6)

Photoshop gets updates from time-to-time and all the updates are free to download and install. Keep your copy of Photoshop updated so you don't miss on any exciting new features! It's also important to keep updating Adobe Camera Raw that comes with Photoshop, especially if you work with raw images.

Here's how you can check for any available updates:

In Photoshop, choose **Help > Updates** as shown below:

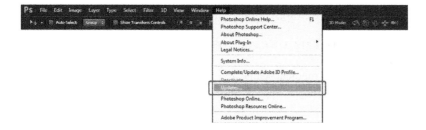

Adobe Application Manager will open and check for any existing updates for you.

If there are any new updates, you are going to see them in here, as shown below:

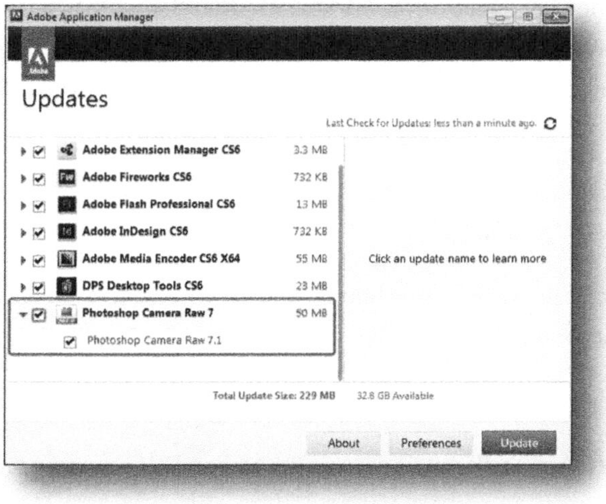

Tick the box next to the update you want to install and click Update.

With Photoshop CC, the updates go through the Creative Cloud.

Adobe Photoshop CC

In May 2013, Adobe made a big announcement. They announced a new release of Photoshop. Just twelve months after releasing Photoshop CS6 Adobe announced **Photoshop CC**. So the way this book is now structured is that it is going to cover Photoshop CC as well.

But first, let me explain some things about **Photoshop CC** and how it's going to work with the future editions of Photoshop because some things have changed.

So turn the page over and start reading about a new generation of Photoshop - **Adobe Photoshop CC**.

Adobe Photoshop CC demystified

Adobe announced that they're going to stop working on what they call 'perpetual licenses' for Photoshop. Basically, there won't be Photoshop CS7. Instead we get Adobe Photoshop CC, part of Creative Cloud. The reason why Adobe are moving towards Creative Cloud based applications is mainly because, in the words of Winston Hendrickson from Adobe:

"The reason behind the subscription-only move is the logistics of supporting two sets of software. We have decided to focus on CC products."

So the changes that are coming with Photoshop CC release mean a few things for Photoshop users (I will clarify some misconceptions here as well):

*   Adobe will keep supporting and updating Photoshop CS6,

*   All new Photoshop features will only arrive at Photoshop CC from now on,

*   New Photoshop CC is subscription only,

*   You can subscribe to just one application, you don't have to subscribe to the entire Creative Cloud (for up to date prices check Adobe website at *www.adobe.com*, as I'm writing this 'Single App subscription' as Adobe calls it is £15 a month),

*   Even though Photoshop CC is a part of Creative Cloud, it doesn't run in your web browser as many people think. You download it and install it on your computer as always.

*   With Photoshop CC you get the updates and new features as soon as they're ready.

*   Adobe Creative Cloud applications can be installed on two computers, both Windows and Mac. However, you can only run one at a time.

For more information on Photoshop CC check Adobe website at *www.adobe.com*.

So if you run Photoshop CC, you will see a slightly different splash screen, something like that:

As there are some differences between Photoshop CS6 and Photoshop CC, whenever you would do something differently in Photoshop CC, whether it's a different dialogue box or different set of options available, or if I want to show you a new feature in Photoshop CC, you're going to see this graphic:

Finally, there's one more thing I want to mention about Photoshop CC. I mentioned Photoshop CS6 Extended earlier in this chapter and some people keep asking me about Photoshop CC Extended. There will be no Photoshop CC Extended, however Photoshop CC will include all the features found in Photoshop Extended, so just one version of Photoshop with the CC release.

Now, you should be ready to start working with Photoshop CS6/CC, so it is time to start with Lesson 1. Enjoy the journey.

Lesson 01

Introducing Photoshop CS6/CC

Things you are going to learn in this lesson are:

- How to set up your computer

- Photoshop CS6/CC interface

- Customising the workspace

- Using Tools panel

- Using Options Bar

- Document management

- Photoshop preferences

- Colour Settings

- History

Computer setup

Before you start working in Photoshop, or even before you install it, you need to make sure that your computer is optimised for Photoshop. Nowadays, almost any computer you buy will be fine for doing some Photoshop work. Obviously, if you plan on doing some more demanding things in Photoshop like working with 3D images, you will need a better, more powerful computer. But for what we are going to do here, almost any computer will be fine. There is less distinction between Mac and Windows computers nowadays. If you have quite a recent computer, it doesn't matter whether you run Windows or Mac. It comes down more to memory and graphics card and both systems are very good, so I'm going to avoid the discussion whether one is better than the other.

There are some minimum requirements for Photoshop CS6, they are:

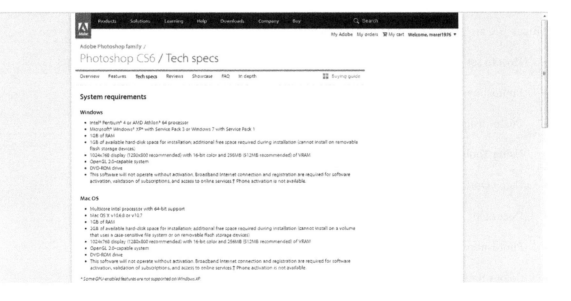

NOTE: The minimum requirements for Photoshop CS6 for RAM memory are 1GB, however I would recommend getting at least 3 or 4GB of RAM. If you have 4GB of RAM or more, you can take the advantage of more memory and run 64-bit version of your operating system and installing 64-bit version of Photoshop. If you run 32-bit operating system, it can only use up to 3.3 - 3.5GB of RAM. However, if you run 64-bit operating system, it can use any amount of RAM you have installed.

Monitor

Choosing a monitor is one of important decisions to make as you are going to spend a lot of time in front of it. The only monitors you can buy nowadays are LCD or LED monitors. These monitors are usually more contrasty as CRT monitors were in the past, which is good. They produce more consistent colour as well as they are digital devices. These monitors can also be calibrated, but I'm not going to go into details here. As to which monitor to choose, it really depends on how big you want it to be (the size will be determined on how far from the monitor you're going to sit).

It goes like this: monitor screen size x 3 = distance, i.e. if you have 20" monitor, you should be sitting 60"(1.5m) from it.

There is one more important aspect of working in Photoshop when it comes to monitors - getting your monitor to display the colours properly. Obviously, you want your images look consistently from one session to another. You also want them to look the same on other monitors, especially on printers' monitors if you're sending images for print.

What you need is a monitor calibration and creating a profile for your monitor. Professional monitors, like Eizo or NEC, come with hardware calibration. However, with most monitors the only adjustments you can make are brightness adjustments.

The only proper way to calibrate your monitor is to use a piece of hardware called a calibrator. There are many calibrators on the market and I am going to show you some more affordable ones as you could spend hundreds of pounds on a calibrator, when you can get a decent calibrator for less than a £100.

Here are two decent calibrators that can be purchased for less than £100:

Colorvision Spyder 4

Spyder 4 lets you calibrate your monitor as well as your Android or iOS tablet and Spyder 4 Express version retails for around £90.

Spyder 4 Pro allows you to calibrate multiple monitors as well as TVs and it retails for around £120.

Pantone Huey

Pantone Huey Pro allows you to calibrate multiple monitors as well and it retails for around £110.

Calibrators measure the output from the monitor. To use a calibrator, first you need to install the software that comes with it. Once you installed the software, you start the application that installed in a process and follow the steps. Software will prompt you to connect the calibrator to a USB port on your computer. Just follow the steps and you will have a display profile installed and ready in a matter of minutes.

Once the display profile is created, it will load into your operating system every time you start your computer. For more details on these two calibrators, follow these links:

Colorvision Spyder website.

Pantone Huey website.

Photoshop Interface

Photoshop CS6 interface has a lot in common with other Adobe Creative Suite 6 applications. And now you can also work with a single application window in Photoshop on both Windows and Mac.

Thanks to the Application Frame on Mac (that's the feature that makes Photoshop's interface on Mac look very similar to the one on Windows), you can work with images that open in tabs.

If you're wondering how to launch Application Frame on Mac, go to Window > Application Frame.

Have a look on the screenshots to see what Photoshop CS6 interface looks like on Windows and Mac.

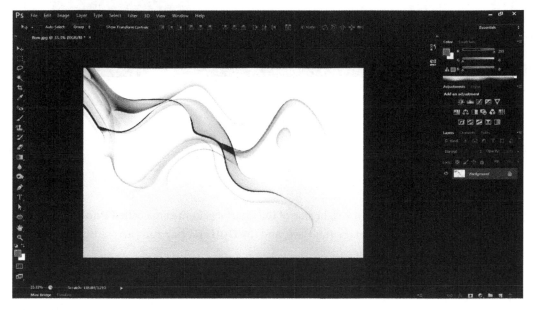

Photoshop CS6 on Windows

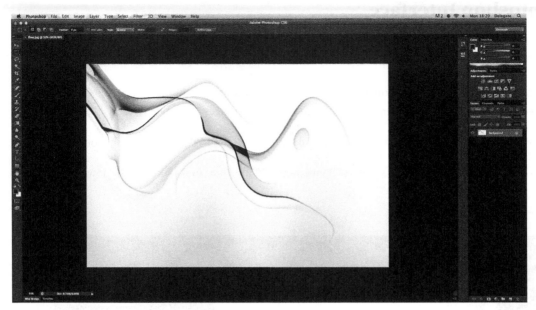

Photoshop CS6 on Mac

Note: Photoshop CC interface looks the same as Photoshop CS6 interface.

All the panels in Photoshop appear on the right side of the interface, in the area called **Panel Dock**. The **Tools panel** appears on the left side of the interface, and the **Options bar** runs across the interface on the top, directly below the application menu.

Customising the Workspace

One of many amazing features in Adobe Photoshop (and other Adobe applications) is the ability to customise the workspace, to make it look the way you want it. Workspaces are created to use alternative layouts and placement of interface elements. Photoshop comes with a set of workspaces to get you started. There are two ways of accessing workspaces:

through the menu: **Window > Workspace**:

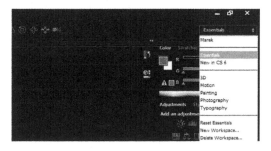

or using the **Workspace Switcher**:

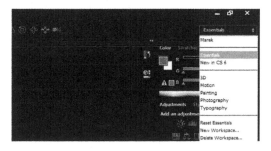

1 Take a moment and look at different workspaces and notice how the Photoshop interface changes, how the panels inside the Panel Dock change.

2 Change the workspace back to Essentials, which is default.

3 For the exercises in our lessons we won't need the Color panel so click and hold on the name of the panel and drag it out from the Panel Dock. When your cursor appears over the document window, release the mouse button:

Color panel now appears as a floating panel.

4 Close the Color panel by clicking the close button (top right corner on Windows, top left corner on Mac).

Back to Panel Dock, you will drop Swatches panel into Adjustments panel.

5 Click and hold on Swatches name and drag the panel into Adjustments panel below. When you see a border around the Adjustments panel, release the mouse button (see next page):

Swatches panel now appears docked with Adjustments panel as shown here:

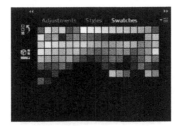

6 You can resize panels by placing the cursor between Swatches panel and Layers panel below and when the cursor changes to double-arrow, click and drag up and down.

7 You can change the position of the panels in a group (in this case Swatches, Styles, and Adjustments) by clicking on the panel's name and dragging it to left or right.

8 It's time to save the workspace. Choose **Window > Workspace > New Workspace...**

9 In **New Workspace** dialogue box type a name for your workspace and click **Save**:

Congratulations! You have successfully created your own workspace. In the next few steps you are going to explore the Tools panel.

Tools panel

Photoshop's Tools panel contains lots of tools, some of them hidden in groups. Any of the tools having a little triangle in the corner contains an expandable group, as shown here:

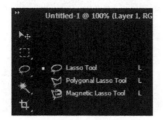

To access tools within a group, click on the tool and hold the mouse button down. In just a second or so the drop-down menu will appear like the one shown above.

Most tools also have keyboard shortcuts assigned to them, one of the letters on the keyboard.

Note: If you don't see the names of the tools and keyboard shortcuts next to them as you mouse over the tools, check your **Preferences > Interface** *category and make sure that the option* **Show Tool Tips** *is selected:*

Because most tools have keyboard shortcuts, you can use keyboard shortcuts to access the tools.

Note: Remember that you may need to hold Shift key with the letter on the keyboard to switch between tools depending on your settings in **Preferences > General** *for* **Use Shift Key for Tool Switch**:

TOOLS PANEL - ADOBE PHOTOSHOP CS6/CC

Note: The Tools panel in Photoshop CC is the same.

10 Give different tools a try using keyboard shortcuts, i.e. V for Move Tool or L for Lasso Tool etc.

Talking about Tools panel and Tools we cannot forget about the Options bar.

Options Bar

Let's start with the position of the Options Bar. Options Bar appears near the top of the application frame, on top of the document window:

Options Bar displays the options for your currently selected tool, I like to call Options Bar being *"context-sensitive"*. The reason being that the options inside the options bar change depending on the tool you have selected.

11 Try clicking on different tools on the Tools panel and notice how the Options bar changes.

Sometimes Options bar will display the tick icon and cancel icon like these:

They appear when you use tools or options where you need to either accept or cancel what you have done. An example here is the Transform option (Edit > Transform).

Documents Management

By default, when you open images in Photoshop CS6, they open in tabs (as tabbed windows) and all the images are nested in a group, as shown here:

12 Open at least two images and notice how they open in tabs.

If you don't like your images to appear in tabs, you can change it in your Preferences. Here's how:

13 Open your Photoshop Preferences in Interface category: **Edit > Preferences > Interface** on Windows, **Photoshop > Preferences > Interface** on Mac.

14 Check on uncheck **Open Documents as Tabs** option:

This option allows you to decide whether you want the images to open in tabbed panels or as floating windows.

To switch between the images you just click on the name of the image on the tab (if you use tabbed documents).

Photoshop Preferences

There are loads of options in Photoshop preferences so we will only cover some of the important ones. Preferences can be found under Edit menu on Windows and under Photoshop menu on Mac. There are a number of categories within preferences so if you know which category you're looking for, you can go straight into this category using the menu:

When you close Photoshop, it will create a file for your preferences, so if you want to keep it somewhere safe, here's where you find it:

C:\Users\Username\AppData\Roaming\Adobe\Adobe Photoshop CS6\Adobe Photoshop CS6 Settings
Windows

Users/Username/Library/Preferences
Mac

Let's have a look at some of the important preferences in Photoshop.

General Preferences

15 Open General preferences using **Edit > Preferences > General** on Windows or

Photoshop > Preferences > General on Mac:

- leave the **Color Picker** set to **Adobe** (especially if you work with other Adobe applications as well to keep it consistent);

- set **Image Interpolation** to **Bicubic Sharper (best for reduction)** - best when scaling images down (and you should avoid scaling images up as they will get pixelated). You can always change this in Image Size dialogue box later on as I will explain later.

In Photoshop CC, the default is **Bicubic Automatic** and I would advice to leave it as it is as it gives good results. Bicubic Automatic detects what you're trying to do when resizing the image and will use the best method of interpolation for the situation.

in the **Options** section:

- keep **Export Clipboard** checked - very useful if you want to paste Photoshop clipboard content into another application;

- **Use Shift Key for Tool Switch** - keep it checked if you want to use the Shift key and the letter key on the keyboard to switch between tools, or uncheck it if you want to use just the letter on the keyboard, i.e. L to switch between Lasso tools (I always keep it unchecked);

- keep **Resize Image During Place** checked - when you place an image in Photoshop using File > Place... you will get bounding box around the image so that you could resize it at the same time;

- **Animated Zoom** - gives you smoother animated zoom when zooming in and out on images using Ctrl++/Ctrl+- or Cmd++/Cmd+-. You will need a graphics card that supports OpenGL for this feature to work;

- if you work with a mouse, you can also **Zoom with Scroll Wheel**;

- **History Log** - may be useful if you want to track everything you've done with an image in Photoshop and you can save it as a text file or into the image's metadata.

Interface Preferences

16 Switch to Interface Preferences:

- you can choose the colour of the interface by choosing **Color Theme**;

- with **Auto-Collapse Iconic Panels** you can open and automatically close panels in iconic mode;

- **Show Transformation Values** (new in CS6) - when moving layers, Photoshop will display the values as you move the layer around.

With **Show Transformation Values** you can choose where the values appear, in terms of position towards the cursor, so from the drop-down menu next to **Show Transformation Values** you can choose the position.

File Handling Preferences

17 Switch to File Handling Preferences:

- **File Extension** leave as **Use Lower Case**, especially if you're going to export images for the Web;

- **Save As to Original Folder** - very useful as Photoshop will save the file into the same folder when you use File > Save As...

- **Save in Background** - great new feature in CS6, Photoshop will save the file in the background so when you save the file you won't see the progress bar while saving any more. I love this feature.

- **Automatically Save Recovery Information Every** - another new feature in CS6, Photoshop will save a recovery version of your file, as a PSD, so if Photoshop crashes, when you restart it it will reopen the file so you don't loose it. You can set here how frequently you want Photoshop to save.

- **Prefer Adobe Camera Raw for Supported Raw Files** - with this option checked, supported raw files will open in Adobe Camera Raw.

- **Maximize PSD and PSB File Compatibility** - use it if you will be opening your PSD files in older versions of Photoshop or in other applications that support PSD file format, like Lightroom. If you don't maximise compatibility and open a PSD file from Photoshop CS6 in Photoshop CS, some layers may not be interpreted correctly.

Performance Preferences

18 Switch to Performance category:

This section of Photoshop's Preferences defines how efficiently is Photoshop going to run.

- **Memory Usage** - set the amount of RAM that Photoshop will use (ideally 60-75% of your RAM). You can use the slider or you can type the value in. The amount of RAM you see as Available RAM is the amount of memory that's left after all the applications that run used their own portion of RAM (including your operating system);

- **History States** in History & Cache section - you can tell Photoshop how many steps to remember as you work on images (the default is 20)

- **Scratch Disks** - Photoshop can use scratch disks (disks connected to your computer) as an extension to RAM memory. Quite often Photoshop creates "mirrors" of content from RAM on the scratch disks. Scratch disks are also used when Photoshop runs out of space in RAM memory, which results in slower performance.

- For best performance use fast hard drive as a scratch disk, like SSD, and a separate hard drive from the one running your operating system and Photoshop.

19 Leave all the other categories in Photoshop Preferences on their defaults and click OK. You're done here.

20 To make sure that all the preferences have been saved close and reopen Photoshop.

Colour Settings

Once you have set up the preferences, it is time for colour settings. Nowadays my guess is you are using a good quality LCD or LED monitor (I don't remember the last time I saw CRT monitor, it's been years since I saw one). Now that you have a good monitor, it is time to set up colour settings in Photoshop.

Setting colour settings is one the first things you should do in Photoshop and that's why I'm covering it here in the first chapter. The defaults are set for specific region like North America.

21 Open Color Settings dialogue box by choosing **Edit > Color Settings** (or use

Ctrl+Shift+K/Cmd+Shift+K):

22 You can use one of the presets in the drop-down menu which are region-specific, i.e. Europe General Purpose, Europe Prepress etc.

Note: Europe General Prepress preset uses Coated FOGRA39 CMYK colour profile, which is a default for printing in Europe.

23 If you live in North America, choose **North America Prepress**, in Europe choose **Europe Prepress**.

24 Uncheck **Ask When Opening** next to Profile Mismatches so that Photoshop won't prompt you every single time you open a file that uses a different color profile.

25 When you uncheck Ask When Opening, the preset drop-down menu changes to custom:

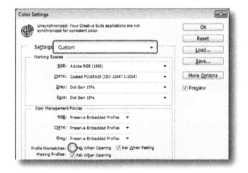

26 Save your changes as a preset by clicking **Save** button.

27 Give your preset a name and save it. You can add comment as well.

Note: Once you set up the colour settings in Photoshop, if you use other Adobe applications, you may want to synchronise your colour settings to other applications. As you may have noticed in the Color Settings dialogue box it reads Unsynchronized on the top of the dialogue box. You can use Adobe Bridge to synchronise the colour settings across the entire Adobe Creative Suite.

History Panel

History panel, as all other panels, can be found under Window menu if it doesn't appear on your screen. History is an important feature incorporated into Photoshop as it allows you for multiple undoes during your working session.

As you work on an image, Photoshop registers all your steps in history. Here's an example:

28 Open an image if you have nothing open.

29 In Layers panel on the right side of your screen double-click on the Background layer.

30 When New Layer dialogue box opens, click OK.

31 Choose **Image > Auto Tone**.

32 Choose **Image > Adjustments > Black & White...** and click OK.

33 Choose **Window > History** to open the History panel:

History panel displays all the steps of the process (to a limit as you set it up in Photoshop Preferences, the default is 20). Using History panel you can access the steps (you can also use the menu: **Edit > Step Backward** or **Edit > Step Forward**). To go back a step (or more), just click on the step in the History panel.

As you can see in the History panel, Photoshop creates an initial snapshot of your image or design (at the top of the History panel):

Snapshots are used for recording what the image looks like in its current state and are great because remember that Photoshop will only remember the last 20 steps by default, so as you keep working on an image, the beginning steps will start disappearing.

You can create additional snapshot by clicking the Snapshot button at the bottom of the History panel (the icon that looks like a camera):

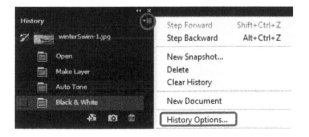

You can also tell Photoshop to create new snapshots every time you save your document. Here's how:

34 Navigate to the History panel's menu (top right corner of the panel), and choose

History Options...:

35 In History Options panel, you can check **Automatically Create New Snapshot**

When Saving (I leave it unchecked):

Note: There are no limits to the number of snapshots that you can create.

That's it for the first lesson! You've learn quite a bit already and it's time to start doing some real work with images inside Photoshop CS6/CC.

Let's move on to Lesson 2.

Lesson 02

Basics of Image Creating and Painting

Things you are going to learn in this lesson are:

- Differences between Vector and Bitmap graphics

- Image Resolution

- Image Interpolation

- Different File Formats

- Creating New Documents

- Working with Backgrounds

- Colourising Images

Vector vs Bitmap Graphics

Digital images (bitmaps) are composed of rectangles of colour in a grid called pixels (short for pixel elements). A photograph might comprise millions of pixels but, even so, the image is resolution-dependent, which means that if an image is enlarged too much it looses quality (pixelated).

On the other hand, vector graphics are resolution-independant and can be scaled up and down without any loss of the quality. That's because vector graphics are created with mathematical calculations. If you draw a shape, as an example, vector application like Adobe Illustrator will keep the information about the size, position, colour, etc as a mathematical data.

Here's an example of a bitmap and vector graphic:

source: Wikipedia

Note: With bitmap images, any time you zoom in onto the image more than 100%, the image will look pixelated.

Photoshop is mainly a bitmap editor, however it has some vector tools as well. As an example, type and shape tools in Photoshop CS6/CC are vector tools.

Image Resolution

There is a very common misconception when it comes to describing image resolution and I am going to explain it here. It is the **ppi** vs **dpi** case.

Dpi (which stands for **d**ots **p**er **i**nch) is the misconception I am talking about here. Dpi refers to the resolution of the output device like a printer. However, the term dpi is very often used (confusingly) as a resolution of an image. This is not true because digital imaging devices like cameras and scanners do not produce dots! Only printers produce dots. And it is very common for manufacturers and retailers to use the term dpi describing scanners and other devices. Here's an example from one of the major stores from their website:

Ppi (pixels per inch) is the correct term that should be used for the resolution of an image on a screen. And that's the term Photoshop uses as the image is composed of pixels. Let's check that.

1 Open an image in Photoshop and choose **Image > Image Size...**.

2 In the Image Size dialogue box notice the resolution of the image described as pixels/inch (or pixels/Centimeter).

*Note: I will explain the Image Size dialogue box in Photoshop CS6 first and then in **Photoshop CC**.*

When working on images in Photoshop, you need to make sure that the images you are working with will have enough resolution if you are going to print them.

Here's something you need to remember about. If you are buying a camera, don't make your buying decision on the number of pixels (resolution). A 20 megapixel camera producing images at a resolution of 5000 x 4000 pixels doesn't have to produce great quality images. It's not just a resolution that counts.

However, the resolution is important. If you have an image that is 5000 x 4000 pixels (a 20 megapixel image), this image could potentially be printed as how big? Well, let's look at an example.

3 Open an image (you can open buckingham.jpg from Images folder) and choose **Image >**

Image Size...

4 Uncheck Resample Image and set the Resolution to **300**.

Now that the image has a resolution of 300ppi, it could be printed at 5.6 x 8.5 cm

5 Change the Resolution to **200**.

Now the image could be printed at 8.5 x 12.7 cm. That's how you can find out how big you can print an image. The example we used here is a low resolution image, but your images will have much higher resolutions and print dimensions.

It is often said that images for print should be supplied at a resolution of 300ppi. This is another common misconception. It doesn't hurt to supply a 300ppi image if you are printing it as A4 or A3 print, but if you print a massive poster, you don't need such a high resolution, especially as the file could be as big as 400 or 500 MB!

Now that you know how to check and change the resolution, let me explain the **Resample Image** drop-down menu that you may have noticed at the bottom of the Image Size dialogue box:

Image Interpolation

Image interpolation (or image resampling as it is often called) is used when scaling an image up or down. There are different methods of scaling in Photoshop to suit different situations. But first, where do you find this option?

6 With one of the images open, choose **Image > Image Size...**

7 In the Image Size dialogue box, look at the bottom and find the option **Resample Image**:

There are a number of options available here and selecting the best option will make a difference when scaling images so let me explain what these options do and how they work.

On the next page I will explain all these options on the Resample Image drop-down menu.

Here's what these options do:

Nearest Neighbor - it uses nearest neighbouring pixels, great for increasing the resolution of screenshots.

Bilinear - it was used a lot in the past, in earlier versions of Photoshop. Not used anymore. It uses neighbouring horizontal and vertical pixels.

Bicubic - great for images with smooth gradients, continuous tones.

Bicubic Smoother - great for scaling images up, creating slightly smoother edges as an image is being enlarged.

Bicubic Sharper - great for scaling images down, keeps the edges sharp as an image is being reduced in size.

Bicubic Automatic - this option automatically chooses the best interpolation method when an image is being resized.

Image Size dialogue box in Photoshop CC

Image Size dialogue box has changed with Photoshop CC release. In Photoshop CC, when you open Image Size dialogue box, the first thing you will notice is the preview of the image on the left side:

This is a great new feature in Photoshop CC, because now you can see what the image will look like when you resize it, especially when you upscale the image. Notice that the preview of the image on the left is at 100% view so you can see the actual quality of the image.

But here's another great new feature in Image Size dialogue box. Now, in Photoshop CC, you can resize it! How great is that? You can make it as big as you want and see more of the image preview. Just click in the bottom right corner of the dialogue box and drag to resize it.

Note: You can resize the Image Size dialogue box in Photoshop CC by dragging from any of the corners, not just the bottom right corner.

Another change in Photoshop CC is that now Image Size dialogue box has an additional new option on the **Resample** drop-down menu:

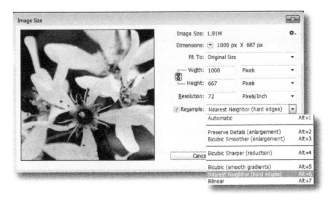

This is a new option that you can see here called **Preserve Details (enlargement)**:

This is a big improvement in Photoshop CC when you need to upscale an image. This used to be a real challenge because as you upscale an image it starts getting pixelated. However, now in Photoshop CC, with **Preserve Details (enlargement)** you can upscale the image with less image quality loss.

I will show you on an example and you can give it a try as well.

Open an image and choose **Image > Image Size...** When Image Size dialogue box opens, increase the Width or Height. I'm going to exaggerate here so that you can easily see the difference, so I'm going to increase the Width of the image by three times:

Now try changing Resample options on the drop-down menu. Try:

• **Bicubic Smoother** (Photoshop up to CS6) and

• **Preserve Details** (new in Photoshop CC).

You will clearly see the difference, especially when it comes to sharpeness on the edges within the image. You may not see it here in print but I can clearly see the difference with this image on my screen:

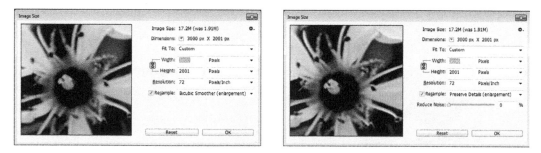

File Formats explained

 PSD - Photoshop Document format - native Photoshop format, saves everything you do in Photoshop. It is a very efficient format when saving images containing multiple layers. It is a proprietary Adobe format.

PSD files can also be used in other Adobe applications like Adobe Dreamweaver and Adobe InDesign, i.e. PSD files can be placed as Smart Objects on web pages in Adobe Dreamweaver.

PSD files can be as big as 2GB and PSD files can handle images up to 30,000 pixels on each side.

 TIFF - Tagged Image File Format - a very well known file format, widely supported. Great format for publishing and archiving. TIFF format can easily be read by many operating systems and applications.

TIFF files can be uncompressed like PSD or you can compress them as well. If you use LZW method when saving a file as a TIFF, it will use a lossless compression (a bit like FLAC in music). JPEG compression offers lossy compression (like a JPEG, which I will explain in just a moment).

 JPEG - Joint Photographic Expert Group - great file format for photographs with very small file size and high compression. JPEG is not suitable for images with text, large blocks of colour, or simple shapes, because crisp lines will blur and colours can shift.

JPG works by analysing images and discarding kinds of information that the eye is least likely to notice.

 PNG - Portable Network Graphics - PNG is an extensible file format for the lossless, portable, well-compressed storage of images. PNG provides a patent-free replacement for GIF and can also replace many common uses of TIFF.

PNG format was designed to replace the older and simpler GIF format and, to some extent, the much more complex TIFF format.

For the Web, PNG really has three main advantages over GIF:

- alpha channels (variable transparency),

- gamma correction (cross-platform control of image brightness), and

- two-dimensional interlacing (a method of progressive display). PNG also compresses better than GIF in almost every case.

 Photoshop PDF - Portable Document Format - PDF was designed for distributing documents that users could open without having any specific (proprietary) software. PDF documents can easily be opened with numerous Free PDF readers.

Creating New Documents

If you are designing from scratch in Photoshop or you want your document some specific dimensions and resolution, the best place to start is the New Document dialogue box.

8 Choose **File > New...** or press Ctrl+N/Cmd+N to open New Document dialogue box:

Inside the dialogue box you can select one of the presets from the Preset drop-down menu:

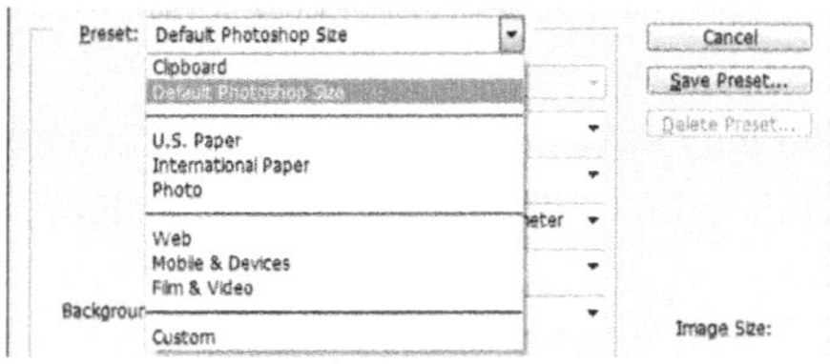

Following Preset drop-down menu are dimensions and resolution of the document and these options change accordingly as you choose a Preset and then Size.

9 From the Preset drop-down menu choose **International Paper**. Notice options that appear next to Size:

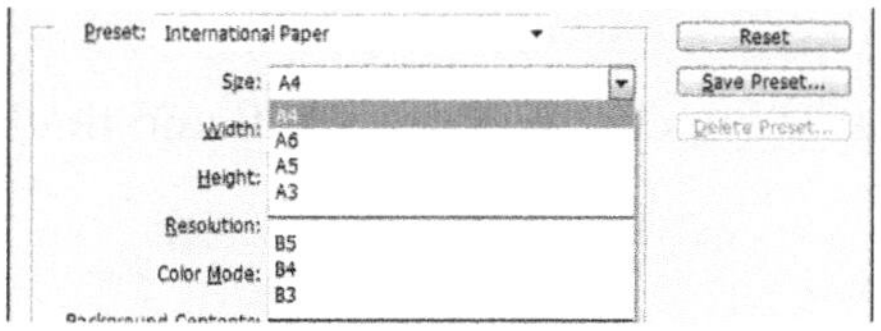

Also notice how the resolution changed to 300 ppi when you set the preset to International Paper.

10 Change the Preset to **Web**. Notice presets for common screen resolutions:

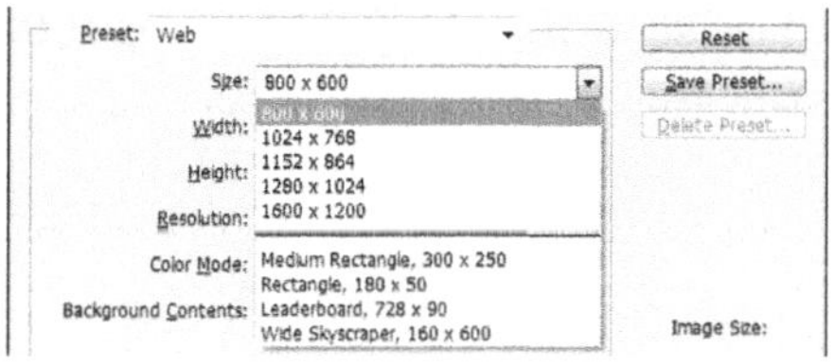

11 Keep Preset set to **Web** and choose **800 x 600**.

12 Resolution should now be **72 ppi**. Check Color Mode, should be **RGB**, and click OK.

A new blank document opens. You may have noticed an option for a background colour inside the New dialogue box. Don't worry if you missed it or if you don't like the colour of your background. I will now show you how to change it.

Working with Backgrounds

If you don't like the background colour of your document, you can easily change it and now you will learn how. We will start with changing the colour of the background by filling the background with another colour.

13 With your new document open, choose **Edit > Fill** and the Fill dialogue box will open:

There are a number of options in here so we'll start simple. Looking at the options inside the Fill dialogue box, we'll start with the Use drop-down menu.

14 Click on the Use drop-down menu to reveal the options as shown here:

Use drop-down menu gives you a choice of what you want to fill your canvas with:

Foreground Color or Background Color or Color...

Let me explain the first two - Foreground and Background Color.

Look at the bottom of the Tools panel. You will find two colour swatches near the bottom like this:

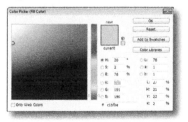

The colour swatch in the front is your Foreground colour and by default it is black. The colour swatch behind is the Background colour and by default it is white. If you want to fill the background with black or white, choose either Foreground Color or Background Color from the drop-down menu. What if you want to use a different colour? That's our next step.

15 Choose **Color...** from the drop-down menu. **Color Picker** opens up like this:

Now, let me explain the **Color Picker**:

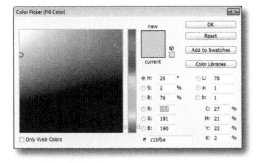

Inside **Adobe Color Picker** you can select colours using four colour models: RGB, CMYK, Lab, and HSB. You can also use hexadecimal values for colour (used in web design). When using one of the colour modes, if you know the colour values you can type them in inside the fields for one of these colour modes, i.e. RGB as 0, 255, 0 to set the colour to green. You can also use the vertical colour slider that appears in the centre of the dialogue box and then click inside the big colour field on the left to choose a particular shade of colour. If you use this method, as you adjust the colour using the color field, the numeric values are adjusted accordingly.

The colour box to the right of the colour slider displays the adjusted colour in the top section and the original colour in the bottom section like this:

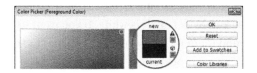

16 Once you've selected the colour, accept it by clicking OK.

17 Back to the Fill dialogue box, click OK to fill the background with your chosen colour.

18 Notice that in the Layers panel on the right side of your screen, the Layer Thumbnail for

the Background layer updated:

As you start building your design with layers, you can always select the Background layer and fill it again with another colour.

Colourising Images

This is one of the questions I get a lot on my Photoshop courses. How do I colourise images? And that's what we're going to do here. Using a graphics tablet like a Wacom tablet will be here of great benefit as with most tasks in Photoshop. I use my Wacom tablet all the time. I actually haven't used a mouse in a very long time.

We're start by adding some colour to a black and white sketch.

19 You can open an image with a sketch if you have it or you can follow along with an image

of a house that you can download from _http://www.sxc.hu/photo/1045581_

20 If you see Missing Profile dialogue box, accept the conversion and click **OK**.

21 In the Layers panel double click on the background layer to unlock it.

22 Name it **Sketch** and click OK.

23 Select **Magic Wand** tool from the Tools panel and in the Options bar make sure that Contiguous is **not selected**:

24 With Magic Wand click once anywhere on the white colour within the image so that everything that is white is selected.

25 Press **Delete** key on the keyboard to delete all white parts of the image:

Now you are ready to start painting different parts of the house with different colours.

26 In the Layers panel click on **Create New Layer** icon (bottom right corner of the Layers panel, little page icon):

27 When new layer appears in the layers panel, click on it, hold the mouse button down and drag it below Sketch layer. When a thick horizontal line appears you can release the mouse button as shown here:

28 Rename the layer by double-clicking on its' name and name it **Paint**. Click OK.

Note: Be careful to double-click on the layer's name. If you double-click next to the layer's name, you will open Layer Styles dialogue box. If this happens, click Cancel and double-click on the layer's name again.

29 Before you start painting make sure that the Paint layer is selected in the Layers panel.

Now you're ready to start painting. You are going to paint on the Paint layer to preserve the original image and if you don't like what you do on the Paint layer, you can always easily hide it or delete it. You just need to set up the Brush tool before you start and that's what you're going to do next.

30 Select Brush tool in the Tools panel.

Brush tool is part of the painting tools - tools that are used for painting or colourising. It works like a traditional drawing tool and it applies colour strokes. First thing you are going to do is to choose the brush and then the size of the brush.

31 Click on the drop-down menu next to the brush size icon:

32 Drop-down menu appears like the one shown here:

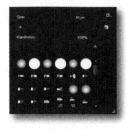

This drop-down menu looks a bit different in Photoshop CC as shown here on the screenshot:

This drop-down menu gives you access to several brush presets/different types of brushes (near the bottom). The **Size** slider is used for adjusting the brush size (up to 5000 px in Photoshop CS6) and the **Hardness** is used for setting the hardness of the brush so that you can make your brush hard, soft, or semi-soft.

Note: You can use keyboard shortcuts to change the size of the brush: the Left Bracket key makes it smaller and the Right Bracket key makes it bigger.

You can also change the hardness of the brush: Shift key and the Left Bracket key makes it softer and Shift key and the Right Bracket key makes it harder.

33 Select a small brush, somewhere in the range of 10 to 20 pixels and set the hardness to 100% to make it a hard edged brush.

34 Zoom in on the image.

35 At the bottom of the Tools panel check what colour is your Foreground colour - that's the colour that Brush tool is going to use. If needed, change it by clicking on the Foreground colour colour swatch.

36 Back to the Options bar, make sure that **Opacity** is set to **100%** so that you can paint with a fully opaque brush:

37 Make sure that the Blend Mode is also set to Normal (default):

Note: Blend Modes for Brush tool can be used for mixing colours with the objects behind. Normal will apply no blending with the objects on the layer below.

38 For now you will use Normal blend mode. Make sure that **Flow** is also set to **100%**:

*Note: **Flow** is a percentage that sets the rate of colour being applied. Each time you press the mouse button the amount of colour applied is controlled by the Flow and it cannot exceed the Opacity percentage unless you click again in the same place.*

39 Now you're ready to start painting. Paint carefully so that you don't go over the edges of the areas to be painted:

40 Once you've done the areas of the same colour, change the Foreground colour and paint other areas.

Note: If you want to, you can apply different colours on different layers.

You can go on and add some other colours, but that's the main concept behind colourising sketches, drawings, etc.

What if you have an image that you want to colourise, but it's a photograph that contains textures and you want to keep them? For example this image:

That's what you're going to do now.

41 Open **red_bus.jpg** from the images folder or open your own image.

42 Duplicate the background layer by choosing **Layer > Duplicate Layer...** and give it a name. Click OK.

43 Keep the newly created layer active.

44 With the new layer selected, select the Brush tool if it's not already selected.

45 Zoom in onto the image (I zoomed in to 100%)

46 In the Options bar choose a small brush and keep Hardness on **100%**.

47 Set Blend Mode to **Normal**, Opacity **100%**, Flow **100 %**:

48 Set Foreground colour to colour you want to use. I will start with red colour for the bus:

If you start painting now, you will notice that a plain colour is being applied to the image, so you need to make a small modification to the Brush tool. This is a technique I have learnt from a friend of mine a number of years ago. It works like a magic.

49 Back to the Options bar, change the Blend Mode of the Brush to **Color**:

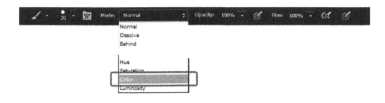

50 Now start painting over the image and notice the difference!

Note: Don't worry if the colour effect is too strong. You are going to reduce the effect in just a moment so keep on painting.

51 Your image should start looking more like this:

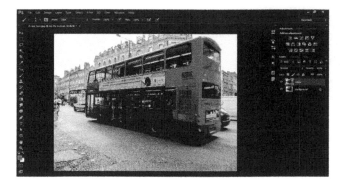

Note: Because you changed the Blend Mode of the brush to Color, you don't have to worry about the areas that are white. If you paint over the sky in the top right corner of the image, nothing happens. That's the beauty of using Blend Modes.

52 Add other colours to the image:

Most probably the colours will be very saturated, so the next step is going to be to reduce the saturation of the colours and blend both layers together for more realistic effect. Because you are working on a separate layer it is going to be simple.

53 Finally, when done, lower the opacity of the top layer to make it blend into the background:

Lowering the opacity of the layer blends it into the layer below because the layer starts getting semi-transparent.

Here's my before-after:

Note: When painting on the image, you can use Shift key to paint in straight lines, i.e.
1) click in one place and release,
2) move the cursor to another location,
3) hold the Shift key down and click again.

This will create a straight line like this:

This is just an introduction to painting, so keep exploring on your own as we move on to next lessons. Just before we move on, to finish this lesson you will save your existing work.

54 Save your work using **File > Save As..** or **Ctrl+S/Cmd+S**.

55 In the Save As dialogue box give your design a name and save it as a **PSD file** if you want to keep the layers:

Notice that whenever you have a document that contains layers, when you save it using File > Save As... Photoshop will try to save it as a PSD file by default. If you're ok with that, you just give file a name and click Save accepting the default.

Also, notice that Layers option will be checked in the same dialogue box, so Photoshop will keep all the layers. And, in the bottom section of the dialogue box, Photoshop will also save the colour profile with the document.

56 Save the file and you're done.

Congratulations. You have successfully finished the lesson. Now you can proceed to the next lesson so turn the page over and see you in a moment in the next lesson.

Lesson 03

Image Editing

Things you are going to learn in this lesson are:

- How Histogram works

- What is Bit Depth?

- Destructive Editing

- Non-Destructive Editing

- Using Levels, Curves, Brightness and Contrast, Shadows and Highlights

- Colour Adjustments

- Using Color Balance

- Vibrance and Hue and Saturation

- Black and White

This chapter is about adjusting or fine-tuning images inside Photoshop CS6/CC. In a later chapter we will talk about adjusting images inside Adobe Camera Raw, but for now we will focus on editing inside Photoshop.

Digital cameras do a great job, producing excellent images. But the resulting photographs will probably need to be adjusted, especially when the lighting conditions change. And that's what we will be doing here in this chapter.

Histogram explained

Before I explain what the histogram is, let's open an image and see what the Histogram looks like.

1 Open an image in Photoshop, you can use **barcelona.jpg** from Images folder.

2 Choose **Window > Histogram**.

3 Histogram panel opens like this:

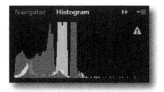

Histogram displays how the pixels are distributed within an image. It shows the number of pixels at each colour intensity level. Histogram shows details in Shadows (on the left), in Midtones (in the middle), and in Highlight (on the right). Thanks to histogram you can decide if the image has enough details for corrections.

Histogram also shows the tonal range of the image. The barcelona image has details concentrated in the shadows and midtones area so it's underexposed. It's an example of an image that would be called "low-key".

Also, as you may have noticed if you used Histogram before, the screenshot I shared with you shows Histogram in Compact Mode.

4 To change it to Expanded View, use the menu in the top-right corner of the panel and choose **Expanded View**:

5 Now you'll see much more information:

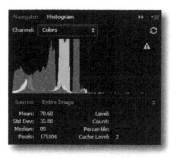

6 If your Histogram looks the same, with colours inside, change Channel drop-down menu to **RGB**:

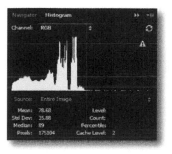

Now you can see the RGB composite, the distribution of the pixels within this RGB image.

Have a close look at the histogram, especially if you are using your own image. If there are peaks that extend above the histogram (in this case it looks like some pixels in the middle - Midtone area), these pixels will be clipped.

7 Now that you've changed the Histogram Channel to RGB, change the view back to

Compact View:

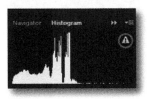

As you can see, Histogram is a very useful feature that can give you an indication of any areas within an image that are clipped. Compact View is great so you can focus on the distribution of the pixels.

While editing image, Photoshop will keep redrawing the histogram and initially Photoshop will use the Histogram's cache. When this occurs, you will see this icon inside the histogram, in the top right corner:

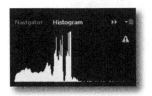

8 If you get this icon, click on this icon to get the Histogram with uncached data.

Photoshop redraws the histogram and updates it.

Bit Depth

What is Bit depth and why are we talking about it here? Let me try to explain Bit depth as simple as possible. Bit depth describes a number of levels in a channel in an image, i.e. 8-bit channel can contain up to 256 tones. Why 256? Here's why: 8 bit is 2^8 which equals 256. Because RGB images contain 3 channels, the images can be 24-bit, i.e. 24-bit (8 bit per channel) JPEGs. Speaking of JPEGs, they're 8-bits per channel files. If you want to use 16-bit per channel files (you can do it with Photoshop), you would need to work with TIFF or PSD files.

Obviously, the higher the bit depth the more information you can work with and the better quality images you can get (bigger tonal range). Since JPEGs are only 8-bit per channel, what other option do you have, you may ask? The answer is Raw. Most DSRL cameras capture raw files at 12-bit (some even 14 bit, like for example my Canon EOS 7D). Since the camera captures 14-bit of data, you should be working with 16-bit files to keep all the data from the camera.

Quite often on online forums I see people arguing if it's worth it to work with 16-bit if most people can't tell the difference between images edited in 16-bit and 8-bit. However, I think that if we can use 16-bit then why not? You never know what you're going to use your images for. If possible, work with the best possible high-quality images. That's why I only shoot raw on my digital cameras.

Note: Not all Photoshop commands are available for 16-bit files, but most are. All commands work with 8-bit images. Many filters only work in 8-bit mode.

One of the big advantages of working with 16-bit images, particularly when adjusting images, is that when using Levels or Curves (which we will cover soon) the signs of loss of pixels will be much more visible in 8-bit images (like barcelona image here). 16-bit images preserve more tonal values than 8-bit images.

Let me show you the difference on an example.

9 Here's an example of a 16-bit image that has been adjusted:

10 Here's the same image converted to 8-bit and adjusted with the same adjustment:

Notice the difference in the histogram. 8-bit image lost a lot of details as represented by gaps in the histogram.

Note: Whenever image loses details after being edited, the histogram displays gaps.

Image Adjustments

There are two approaches to image adjustments.

First, the old way, is to apply adjustments directly to the image (destructive way) via **Image > Adjustments** menu. Direct image adjustments may be a good solution if you don't need the flexibility of having editable layers or if you want to quickly edit an image, save it and export it and you won't need it again.

Second approach is via **Adjustment Layers**. Adjustment layers have many fantastic features like:

- they are editable,

- they are not permanent and non-destructive,

- they can be masked,

- they are vector based,

- they don't increase the file size.

To access Adjustment layers, you can use the **Adjustments panel**, which can be found under **Window > Adjustments**.

11 Open Adjustments panel if it's not already open.

Adjustments Panel

The Adjustments panel displays all available non-destructive adjustments (not all adjustments are available as adjustment layers, but most are). You can click any of the icons to apply an adjustment as a non-destructive adjustment layer (you are going to do it in just a moment). As you move the cursor over the icons, the names of the adjustments will appear in the top-left corner of the panel:

Adjustments available in the Adjustments panel are (in rows, starting from the top row):

- **Brightness/Contrast, Levels, Curves, Exposure, Vibrance,**

- **Hue/Saturation, Color Balance, Black & White, Photo Filter, Channel Mixer, Color Lookup,**

- **Invert, Posterize, Threshold, Selective Color, Gradient Map**

Let's start adjusting the image so that you can see how they work.

Levels Adjustment

12 In the Adjustments panel click the Levels adjustment icon:

Properties panel opens (new in Photoshop CS6) with the Levels adjustment options.

Levels adjustment is one of the most popular adjustments in Photoshop and it has been for a long time. In a later chapter we are going to cover Adobe Camera Raw and if you use Camera Raw for editing images before you bring them into Photoshop, you probably won't need to use Levels. However, if you plan on doing all the work inside Photoshop, it's good to know how Levels work.

Here's what Levels controls look like inside the Properties panel:

In the centre of the Properties panel you can see the histogram, like the one in the Histogram panel. Looking at the histogram inside the Levels you can tell that the image is too dark and lacks contrast (biggest concentration of pixels appears on the left side of the histogram and in the centre). There is a number of things you can do here. Let me show you a few techniques.

13 Directly below the histogram there are three sliders: black, grey and white. They represent shadows, midtones and highlights. Click on the white slider and start dragging it to the left:

Notice how the image gets brighter as you're moving the highlights slider to the left. Levels often have a big impact on the image, quite often Levels adjustment may be all you need when working on an image.

14 Keep the Properties panel with the Levels open. Try something else. As you drag the

highlights slider, hold the **Alt/Opt** key down:

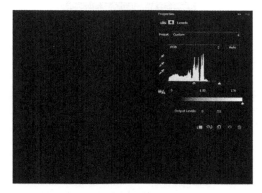

What's happening here is when you hold the Alt/Opt key down as you drag the highlights slider, Photoshop will initially show the image in black in what's often called "threshold display mode". The light points that start appearing when you move the slider to the left started showing where clipping could occur. So what you want to do here is move slider as far as where the light points start appearing, but not too far.

15 Move slider to the point where light points start appearing (more than just one):

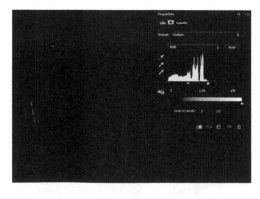

16 Release the Alt/Opt key and the mouse button and check what the image looks like:

It looks pretty good. Not perfect yet, but it's a good starting point. With the black slider (shadows), we could probably leave it as it appears directly under the histogram:

17 Give it a try and move the shadows slider slightly to the right with the Alt/Opt key down.

18 When the clipping appears, release the Alt/Opt key and mouse button

Now it's time for the grey slider - midtones. With grey slider you can adjust the contrast within the image, this slider adjusts gamma within an image. It changes the intensity of the midtones. Our image looks good so far, but it may look even better once we adjust the contrast.

19 Start moving the midtones slider and notice how the image changes.

Notice how the image totally changes when you move the midtones slider:

20 Adjust the midtones slider to your liking so that the image look good.

21 Because you used an adjustment layer, you can edit the adjustment at any time. Just open the Properties panel and make sure that you have the Layers layer selected:

If you don't like the adjustment and you don't need it anymore, you can delete it. Here's how you can do it.

22 Click on the Levels layer in the Layers panel, hold the mouse button down, and drag it on top of the bin icon at the bottom of the Layers panel:

There's another way of deleting a layer:

23 Undo the last step using **Edit > Step Backward**.

24 With the Levels layer selected, right-click on it and choose **Delete Layer**.

Curves Adjustment

Curves is yet another very useful and very popular adjustment in Photoshop. I use Curves quite a lot but I do use Levels from time to time as well. Levels are easier to use and are great for a quick adjustment. As with most things in Photoshop, there are many ways of achieving certain effect. Adjustments you did with Levels can be done with Curves as well. Curves adjustment gives you more control over the tonal balance of the image when compared to Levels. And there's a great tool inside Curves that I love using and I'm going to share it with you here.

With Curves adjustment, you can target specific points within the tone curve and you're not limited to three sliders that appear inside the Levels adjustment.

24 In the Properties panel click on the Curves adjustment icon:

This opens Curves adjustment in the Properties panel:

The curve inside Curves adjustment represents the tonal range of the image. The horizontal axis represents the input values and the vertical axis the output values.

Near the top of the panel, there is a channel drop-down menu, which by default is set to RGB or CMYK composite, which means all the channels will be affected when changes are being applied.

You can use this drop-down menu to target one of the channels (something I often use for colour correcting, more on that later).

The sliders below the histogram work in the same way here as they do in Levels, so you can use Alt/Opt key for threshold view mode that I explained earlier in this chapter.

Here's where the fun begins. In Curves you can manipulate the curve inside the histogram and edit the tonal range of the image in this way. Let's give it a go.

25 Inside the Curves click in the centre of the curve and drag it up to brighten the image:

26 Or you can drag down to darken the image, depending on the image you are working on.

But there is an easier, and more fun way to use the Curves. Let me show you that in the next step.

Instead of clicking and dragging on the curve, you can use my favourite tool inside Curves, that arrived in Photoshop from Adobe Photoshop Lightroom. You can use that to adjust the image while clicking on it. Sounds great, doesn't it? Well, it is great. Let me show you that 'magic' tool.

27 Click the Targetted Adjustment Tool (TAT tool) or On-image adjustment tool as it's often called icon inside Curves as shown here:

28 Move the cursor over the image and notice how a circle appears over the histogram (I place the cursor over the sky):

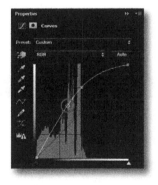

This circle shows you where this part of the image appears on the tone curve. If you click, this will add a point on a curve.

29 Click on the image and notice how your cursor changes to a hand.

Now to adjust the image, you can simply click and drag on the image with the tool.

30 Hold the mouse button down and drag to adjust the image. This is so much fun!

Use this technique to make parts of the image lighter and darker. You can click and drag on the image a number of times, in different parts of the image, and Photoshop will keep creating points on the curve automatically.

Note: Did you notice that when you selected the TAT tool inside Curves, the Options bar changed?

When the TAT tool is active, Options bar displays the Sample Size drop-down menu where you choose the sampling size:

31 If the Sample Size is set to Point Sample, change it to a bit bigger to make it easier to average the reading from the sample on the image (I usually use 5 by 5 average).

32 If you clicked and dragged on the sky, like I did, it's time to adjust the shadows as well.

Click and drag on the lamps to adjust the shadow areas within the image:

The image starts looking better. What I would recommend here is adjust the image the way you like it. Remember that some people prefer images that are more contrasty while others like their images having less contrast. So my advice is, adjust image to your liking.

33 My final curve looks like this:

Before we move on, let me explain a few more things inside the Properties panel. Or precisely, the icons at the bottom of the Properties panel:

Starting from the left:

Clipping the Adjustment layer - by default the Adjustment layer applies to every layer below inside the Layers panel. However, if you want it to apply to only one layer, you can clip the Adjustment layer (more on that later).

Previous State - you can click on this icon to see before (previous) state of the image.

Reset - you can reset back to the adjustment's defaults if you're not happy with the effect you've achieved.

Layer visibility - you can turn the layer visibility on and off.

Delete - you can delete the adjustment layer.

Curves Presets

If you are curious like myself (and George) and if you started exploring the Curves adjustment dialogue box, you may have found Curves presets already. They reside in the top section of the dialogue box.

34 Click the Preset drop-down menu to reveal the presets:

The drop-down menu contains a number of presets that come with Photoshop. It can contain any presets you or someone else have created and saved. Some of these presets are pretty simple like making image lighter or darker, others are more sophisticated like Cross Process or Negative.

35 Go through different presets on the drop-down menu and notice how the image changes.

36 If you don't like any of the presets, undo to go back to your adjustment.

Brightness and Contrast

Brightness and Contrast adjustment has been in Photoshop for as long as I remember (and probably even longer than that). This adjustment is not as sophisticated as Curves or even Levels (as you will see in just a moment), but it's just another option to take into consideration when editing images. It is very easy to use, that's for sure.

37 In the Layers panel, click on the eye icon next to the Curves adjustment layer to hide it for a moment:

38 Select the **Background** layer.

39 In the Adjustments panel click the **Brightness and Contrast** adjustment icon:

40 When the Brightness and Contrast adjustment opens in the Properties panel, you'll see just two sliders, as shown here:

The sliders for Brightness and Contrast are self-explanatory as you can see from their names.

41 Use the sliders to improve the tonality of the image and see if you can get close to what you achieved with Levels or Curves.

I've managed to achieve a pretty good result, pretty much similar to Levels, by setting the sliders as shown here on the screenshot:

Note: I'm often asked about Use Legacy option at the bottom of the Brightness and Contrast adjustment. Use Legacy option is available here because when Adobe released Photoshop CS3, they changed the default behaviour of Brightness and Contrast, and Use Legacy option is here for maintaining compatibility with images that could have been edited with the 'old' Brightness and Contrast adjustment or could have been used in a recorded action.

Big Thank You to Martin Evening for explaining Use Legacy option in one of his books.

Before we move on to colour adjustments, there is one more useful adjustment to cover - Shadows/Highlights.

Shadows and Highlights

Shadows/Highlights is one of these few adjustments that are not available in the Adjustments panel (as you may have noticed already). Because of that, you are going to duplicate the image layer so that you don't work on the original.

42 Start by opening **plane.jpg** from Images folder (or use your own image).

43 Choose **Layer > Duplicate Layer...** (or right-click on Background layer and choose Duplicate Layer...)

44 Name the new layer **Shadows/Highlights** and click OK.

45 With the new layer selected, choose **Image > Adjustments > Shadows/Highlights...**

Initially Shadows/Highlights adjustment opens in basic mode that looks like this:

You can access more options by ticking **Show More Options** box in the bottom left corner.

Shadows and Highlights adjustment is great when you want to bring back more details in shadows or highlights and quite often it performs magic. Shadows and Highlights works by comparing neighbouring pixels within the image and creates adjustments based on average pixel values within the area.

Shadows and Highlights options explained:

Amount - the amount of shadows or highlights correction.

Tonal Width - the tonal range of pixels that will be affected by the adjustment.

Radius - the width of the area that's being analysed (in pixels).

I think it's best if you just use these to get your head around the options.

46 In the Shadows/Highlights dialogue box click **Show More Options** if you haven't done it already.

The settings you use will depend on the image you are working with. Keep in mind that when you adjust the shadows, if you use too big a Radius, this will average a big selection of pixels and most of the pixels within the image may be lightened. On the other hand, if you use too small a Radius, this may lighten the midtones as well. I often use Radius that is more or less half of the value of the Amount. Let's put it to practice.

47 Set the Amount to **40%** and Radius to **20 px**.

Note: The way the sliders are organised, like most options in Photoshop, is the way you should be adjusting them. In this case, you should adjust Amount and Tonal Width first, and then adjust the Radius.

Remember that the Radius value will depend on how big are the light and dark areas within the image.

48 Move the **Tonal Width** slider (Shadows) and notice how the shadows change.

49 Keep adjusting the sliders in Shadows section until you're happy with the effect.

50 In Highlights section (focusing on the sky), increase Amount to **27%** or so.

51 Increase Tonal Width to about **70%** and Radius to **30 px**.

By now the image should look much better than before. You can keep on adjusting the options to get the desired effect.

52 When you're done, click OK to accept the settings.

Because the Shadows and Highlights adjustment is not within the Adjustments panel, Photoshop didn't create an adjustment layer. Because of that, you won't be able to re-edit the adjustment. Here's what I mean.

53 With the Shadows/Highlights layer selected, choose **Image > Adjustments > Shadows/Highlights**.

54 When the Shadows/Highlights dialogue box opens, notice that Photoshop doesn't

remember any of your settings:

This is the big difference between using the Adjustment layers and using the Image > Adjustment menu. And that's the reason why you duplicated the background layer before you applied Shadows and Highlights.

When you re-apply the adjustment, as you did in the last step, Photoshop resets the adjustment back to the defaults.

55 Click **Cancel** to cancel the dialogue box.

Another possibility when editing images, something I don't personally use, is to use Auto adjustments. They can be found under Image menu and there are three here: Auto Tone, Auto Contrast, and Auto Color.

56 Close the file.

Colour Correction

We have done quite a bit on image editing, using some of the adjustments inside Photoshop. Now it is time for some colour correcting/colour editing.

Look at the image below that represents the Colour Wheel so that you can get an idea on how the colours relate to each other.

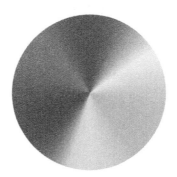

An obvious choice when editing colours seems to be the Color Balance adjustment, so we'll start with it.

Color Balance

Color Balance adjustment seems to be the first one that intuitively gets chosen for colour correction, however is not the only choice. It is a very simple and intuitive adjustment and can be applied as a non-destructive adjustment layer.

57 Open **hotel.jpg** from Images folder (or use your image if you prefer).

58 Let's quickly adjust the tonal range of the image. In the Adjustments panel click on **Levels** adjustment.

59 Adjust the image and close the Properties panel.

60 Add **Color Balance** adjustment:

61 When Color Balance adjustment opens inside the Properties panel, use the sliders to adjust the colours.

If you're using the hotel image, this image has a slight cyan/green tint, so use the Cyan/Red or Magenta/Green slider.

62 You can add some yellows to this image to make it a big warmer as well:

By now you should have (at least) 2 adjustment layers in your Layers panel. Because you have been working with Adjustment layers, you can edit them at any time, as you already know, by highlighting an adjustment layer and checking the Properties panel. Remember that to keep all the layers you will need to save the file as either PSD or TIFF (in case you want to save it now).

Now, let's move on to some other adjustments, like Levels.

Colour Correction with Levels

Levels may not seem like a good adjustment for colour correction, but there are some interesting features within Levels. As you may have remember, Levels adjustment has the channel drop-down menu. You can use that for some colour correction.

63 First, hide all the adjustment layers and select the layer with the image:

64 In the Adjustments panel click the Levels adjustment icon.

65 When the Levels 2 open inside the Properties panel, change the channel drop-down menu to **Green**:

66 Move the **Midtones** slider to the right to bring some more reds into the image.

67 Switch to the **Blue** channel and move the **Midtones** slider to the right to bring in some more yellows into the image.

Note: If you're wondering why you were using the Blue channel to add more yellows to the image, check the colour wheel earlier in this chapter. Notice that blue and yellow are on the opposite sides of the colour wheel. The same with the Green channel - on the opposite side from green there is magenta.

68 If you want to see what the image looked like before you adjusted it, you can click on the eye icon next to the Levels 2 layer to hide it.

Colour Correction with Curves

Now, this is the adjustment I would normally use for colour correction. You are going to see why in just a moment.

69 Open **battersea.jpg** from the images folder.

70 Select the layer with the image and add a Curves adjustment layer.

71 When Curves open inside the Properties panel, target the Green channel:

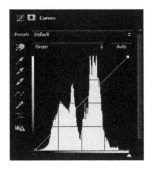

The image has a green cast and that's why you're targetting the green channel.

You can also adjust the input sliders as you did previously with the Curves by dragging the shadows and highlights sliders inwards. I moved them slightly inwards until they started clipping.

72 Click in the middle of the green channel and drag slightly down and to the right to remove the green colour cast:

Note: You can use keyboard shortcuts to access channels inside Curves:

Alt/Opt + 2 - Composite RGB or CMYK

Alt/Opt + 3 - Red (or Cyan)

Alt/Opt + 4 - Green (or Magenta), and so on.

Vibrance

Vibrance is an interesting adjustment, present in Photoshop as well as in Adobe Camera Raw. It is quite similar to the Saturation, however Vibrance is more subtle. Vibrance only increases the saturation of the colours that are not saturated already. The colours that are saturated get no increase of the saturation when Vibrance is being used. Vibrance also keeps the skin tones protected from being too saturated.

Both options, Saturation and Vibrance, are available inside the Vibrance dialogue box, but you are going to use Vibrance only most of the time.

73 Apply the Vibrance adjustment to the battersea image as an adjustment layer.

74 Increase the Vibrance to boost the colours within the image.

75 Apply Vibrance to other images as well, like hotel image we worked on earlier.

Here's my before (on the left) and after (on the right):

Hue and Saturation

Our final colour adjustment in this chapter is Hue and Saturation. You can use Hue and Saturation to adjust the colours, using Hue, Saturation, and Lightness sliders. You can also increase or decrease the saturation of all the colours in the image, making it a black and white image as an example, or you can shift the colours within the image.

Let's open the adjustment and I will explain the options.

76 With the hotel image still open, add a Hue and Saturation adjustment as an adjustment

layer.

Hue and Saturation allows you to target the entire RGB composite or one of the colour ranges. Let's put it in practise.

77 Start moving the **Hue** slider and notice how the colours within the image shift:

Here are three examples of shifting the hue (original on the left):

This is one of examples of using Hue and Saturation for creative effects. With just one slider you can totally change the colours within an image. Let 's do one more example of using Hue and Saturation on another image for another interesting effect.

78 Open **barcelona.jpg** from Images folder.

79 From the Adjustments panel add **Hue and Saturation** adjustment.

80 Inside Hue and Saturation adjustment start moving the Hue slider and notice how the colour of the sky changes:

81 You can close the file.

As with all things Photoshop, keep experimenting and searching for new ways of creating interesting effects. Also, as you may have already noticed, you can stack adjustments used as adjustment layers. We have added quite a few and they all apply to the image below.

Black and White

Black and White is our last subject in this lesson on editing images. Black and White has always been close to my heart as when I started getting into photography around age 14-15, I remember getting into developing my images in the darkroom I would make in our bathroom at home. At that time, black and white was the only option if you wanted to develop your own films and photos (nowadays you can use a good inkjet printer to print your own images in colour or black and white). And as we are now in the digital age of photography, I still love black and white, especially for portraits and landscapes.

Let me start by saying that even if you are going to work with black and white images, my tip for you here will be to shoot in colour. Don't set up your camera to shoot in black and white. Convert images to black and white in Photoshop or Camera Raw.

One way to convert images to black and white is to use grayscale conversion using **Image > Adjustments > Desaturate**. However, this option doesn't give you any control over the conversion so I wouldn't use that. Not that it is a bad adjustment, it's just that I like having some control over how the images are edited and converted.

82 Open **alps.jpg** from the Images folder.

83 Give desaturating a go using **Image > Adjustments > Desaturate**.

The image doesn't look too bad, but it lacks contrast and it doesn't really have any depth in it.

84 Undo the last step using **Edit > Step Backward**.

A much better way of converting images will be to use Black and White adjustment, which can be found in both the Adjustments panel and Image > Adjustments menu.

85 Add a **Black and White** adjustment layer:

86 Black and White adjustment layer opens in the Properties panel:

When using Black and White adjustment Photoshop gives you access to the full use of RGB during the conversion, unlike Desaturating. Even with the default conversion inside Black and White adjustment the image looks good. But you can make it look much better.

Let's let Photoshop apply an auto conversion and analyse the image colours.

87 Click **Auto** button inside Black and White adjustment.

Now the image looks much better, even with just a click on the Auto button. I often use the Auto button as a starting point in black and white conversion. You can see that the image now looks much better than when you used Desaturate.

88 If you are not happy with the effect, use sliders to adjust the black and white conversion.

In this example, here's what I did: I increased **Yellows**, decreased **Cyans** and **Blues**:

Note: Black and White adjustment also contains the Target Adjustment Tool (TAT tool) like Curves adjustment, so you can make adjustments directly on the image instead of using the sliders. You will find the TAT tool in the top left corner of the Properties panel.

Black and White Presets

Another option to consider when converting images to black and white using the Black and White adjustment is to use the presets that come with the adjustment. Black and White adjustment has Presets menu in the top section:

I love these presets as they simulate the behaviour of filters we used to use on the lens when shooting on black and white film. For example, I remember using red and blue filter on the lens for increasing the contrast between different colours within the scene. Now, you can recreate these effects with the presets inside the Black and White adjustment.

89 Try different presets on the image.

90 If you don't find a preset that creates the effect you're after, use the sliders like you did earlier.

91 With sliders adjusted, create a new preset for re-use in the future by clicking on the menu button in the top right corner of the Properties panel.

92 From the menu choose **Save Black & White Preset...**

93 Give your preset a name and save it.

94 Close the file.

And that's how you can convert your colour images to black and white with the help of the Black and White adjustment in Photoshop. Congratulations on completing the lesson.

Lesson 04

Image Retouching

Things you are going to learn in this lesson are:

- Cloning with Clone Stamp tool

- Refining the edges with Eraser tool

- Retouching with Clone Stamp tool

- Healing Brush tool

- Spot Healing Brush tool

- Patch tool

- Content-Aware Fill

- Content-Aware Move tool (New in CS6)

- Portrait Retouching

Image retouching is what most people associate Photoshop with. Most people coming on my Photoshop courses want to learn how to retouch their images and as we start going through retouching techniques, the most popular comment from delegates is "I'm going to retouch all my images tonight!".

And that's what we're going to go cover in this chapter. Retouching, cloning, etc.

Clone Stamp tool

As in the name of the tool, Clone Stamp tool clones pixels within the image. You can use Clone Stamp tool to copy an object from one image to another (or from one layer to another). And that's exactly what you're going to do here.

Here's how the Clone Stamp tool works:

1. you hold down Alt/Opt key and click once to set the source point (i.e. a clean part of the image);

2. you release Alt/Opt key;

3. move the cursor to the location that needs to be retouched and click or click and drag to start cloning.

Let's put it to practise. You are going to remove a cable from the image.

1 Open **cable.jpg** from Images folder.

2 Create new layer by clicking in a New Layer icon at the bottom of the Layers panel (or using Layer > New Layer menu).

3 With the new layer selected, choose **Clone Stamp** tool from the Tools panel:

4 In the Options Bar set the size of the brush for Clone Stamp (like with Brush tool).

5 Also in the Options Bar, set the brush to about 50% hardness:

Note: If you're using the same image and not your own, set the brush to about 20 px.

In **Photoshop CC**, options for brush look a bit different:

In **Photoshop CC**, you get this preview of the brush in the top left corner, which you can actually use for changing the shape of the brush. You can just click and drag on these points on the circle.

6 Leave **Blend Mode** as Normal, **Opacity** 100% and **Flow** 100%.

7 Leave **Aligned** checked and set **Sample** to All Layers:

If you're wondering what Aligned and Sample do, let me explain.

When Aligned is checked, Photoshop will keep connection between the sampling point and the area where you're retouching. As an example, if you move the cursor to the right after you've sampled, the sampling point will move to the right as well.

Sample allows you to choose where you want to sample from. If you set it to All Layers, you can work on a blank layer, as you're going to do here, and keep sampling from the bottom layer.

8 Zoom into 100% view or even 200% depending on your screen size.

9 Position the cursor next to cable on the floor (that's where you're going to sample from).

10 Hold Alt/Opt key down and click to sample:

Note: Notice how your cursor changes when you hold Alt/Opt key down.

11 Release the mouse button and Alt/Opt key.

12 Move the cursor over the cable and start painting over it:

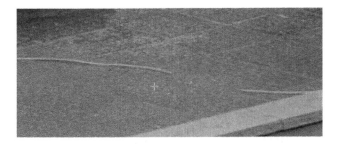

And that's where the magic happens! As you start painting over the cable, it will start disappearing. Notice the crosshair symbol next to the cable and notice how it's moving as you paint over the cable. That's your sampling point. That's where the Clone Stamp tool is sampling from.

At any time, you can release the mouse button and start painting in another location, or you can resample again in another location using Alt/Opt key and click.

13 Keep on cloning until the cable is gone.

Before (on the left) and after (on the right).

Note: When removing the cable from the door, sample from the door next to the cable for best results.

Clone Stamp tool is great for cloning pixels and can be used for removing objects from the background, however, keep in mind that it just clones the pixels. It doesn't blend the content so you need to make sure that you sample from a very similar area.

14 Zoom in close to the image and notice a bottle on the floor. Remove it by sampling from the floor are around the bottle (with Alt/Opt) and painting over the bottle.

Because the background around the bottle is a repeating pattern, you can easily use the Clone Stamp tool. This is just one of the examples of using the Clone Stamp tool. The next example that you're going to work on will include cloning an object from one image into another, like cloning a person from one image into another image.

15 Close cable.jpg.

16 Open **plane.jpg** and **santa.jpg**.

To see both images at the same time, as this will help with cloning, you're going to change the arrangement of the documents. You are going to clone the santa onto the plane! How about that?

17 With both images open, choose **Window > Arrange > 2-up Vertical**.

18 On santa.jpg image create a new blank layer and make it active by clicking on it.

19 Zoom both images in to make it easier to work (I zoomed in to 100%):

20 Click on the tab for Santa image to make it active.

21 With Clone Stamp tool selected, hold down Alt/Opt and click on the Santa to sample.

Note: In this example, I'm using a bit bigger brush because santa is bigger.

22 Once you've sampled, click on the tab for plane image and start painting on the plane's wing:

Here's the santa appearing suddenly on the plane's wing! Doesn't it look great?

23 Keep on painting until you get the entire Santa on the wing and don't worry about the background behind the Santa for now.

24 Once you've got the entire santa on the wing, set the windows' arrangement back to default using **Window > Arrange > Consolidate All to Tabs**.

25 Santa now appears on a separate layer, so you can rearrange the Santa by dragging him around with the Move tool.

It's time to remove the background behind the Santa. For now, you are going to do it destructively with the Eraser tool. Later on, we will talk about doing it in a non-destructive way using Layer Masks.

26 From the Tools panel select the Eraser tool:

27 Zoom in very close onto the image.

28 In the Options bar set the size of the brush to very small so that you can be very precise.

29 Leave the Mode set to Brush and both Opacity and Fill set to 100%:

30 Start erasing the background behind the Santa (on the top layer):

31 Go all the way around the santa to remove all the background.

32 Once you've done, reposition the santa with the Move tool.

33 If you need to resize santa, use **Edit > Transform > Scale**.

34 Handles around the image appear, but wait with the resizing.

Before you start resizing, you need to make sure that you don't distort the image. There are a few ways as usual.

- You can hold Shift key and drag from one of the corner handles of the image:

- You can use the Options bar and in the Options bar click on the chain icon, which will keep the proportions, and then just drag from one of the corner handles:

35 Using your chosen method resize the santa.

Note: If you don't see the entire handles around the santa because your santa is close to the top of the image and your image is zoomed in, zoom out a bit.

36 Once you've resized the santa, you need to either accept or cancel the transformation using one of these icons in the Options bar:

The crossed circle icon cancels the transformation and the tick accepts it. You can also press Escape or Enter on the keyboard.

37 Close the file. You can save it if you want to keep it.

As you have seen, Clone Stamp tool can be used for cloning objects from one image into another as well as for retouching images. You wouldn't use it when retouching portraits as it doesn't produce good results with skin tones (because it's just cloning pixels), but you can use for retouching areas like textures, backgrounds, patterns.

Healing Brush Tool

Healing Brush Tool is a bit different from Clone Stamp tool. Healing Brush Tool allows you to correct imperfections in images and make them disappear in the surrounding area of the image. Healing Brush Tool, like Clone Stamp tool, allows you to sample pixels from an image and paint, however with Healing Brush Tool, as you apply the brush strokes, it will match the texture, lighting, and shading of the surrounding pixels and heal the area. As a result of applying Healing Brush Tool, the pixels blend into the area around the cloning area.

Note: If you are using Photoshop Extended, you can also apply Healing Brush tool to video frames and animation frames.

38 Open **cornwall.jpg** from Images folder.

This image has a lot of dust on it, which needs attention. Because the dust appears on the sky area and there are so many different shades and tones within the sky, you wouldn't use Clone Stamp tool here. Healing Brush tool will do a much better job. Healing Brush also reads the pixels just outside the cursor area and calculates how to create a smooth transition within the area you are working on.

Healing Brush tool is not a magic tool. There are a few things you will need to remember when working with this tool. One of the common things Photoshop users discover when working with the Healing Brush is that when you work close to the edge with contrasting pixels, i.e. light and dark pixels, it will create a blend of these pixels which will look a bit like a smudge. Just something to keep in mind. One of the solutions you could apply in this situation would be to use Clone Stamp tool on the edges of contrasty pixels or you could create a selection and apply Healing Brush tool.

39 Duplicate the background layer so that you don't work on the original.

40 Give a duplicate layer a name, i.e. Retouched.

41 With the top layer (duplicate) selected, select Healing Brush tool:

42 Zoom into 100% view.

There is a lot of dust in the image, but you can find areas with no dust and that's where you are going to sample from with the Healing Brush tool.

Before you start using Healing Brush, you'll need to check the Options bar and set some options (like with other tools in Photoshop).

43 In the Options bar set the size of the brush for Healing Brush:

With this image, set the size to around 20px or less and set the Hardness to around 50%. You can also use Pen Pressure option next to Size at the bottom of the dialogue box if you use a Wacom tablet to use the pen pressure.

44 Leave Mode as **Normal** and Source as **Sampled**. Leave **Aligned** unchecked and Sample as **All Layers**:

45 Place the cursor over the "cleaner" part of the sky, hold the **Alt/Opt** key down and click to sample.

Note: Notice how your cursor changes when you hold the Alt/Opt key down.

46 Move the cursor over the area than needs to be tidied up and click and drag or click a few times.

47 Keep on removing the dust from the image until it's all gone.

Note: You can keep Alt/Opt clicking in different parts of the image for sampling from different areas of the image.

Have you noticed that as you were cloning within the image, Healing Brush kept sampling from the same area until you resampled again, even when you released the mouse button and clicked again somewhere else within the image? That's how it works when **Aligned** is unchecked.

If you were to clone the santa from one image into another with the Healing Brush tool, I would suggest checking Aligned to avoid sampling from the same place as this could result in a santa with two or three heads or five arms as an example.

Another option worth explaining is Sample (in the Options bar). There are three options here:

- Current Layer,

- Current & Below,

- All Layers.

The Sample drop-down menu allows you to choose how you want to sample the pixels. You can sample the pixels from the current layer only (**Current Layer** option), which is your selected layer or you can sample pixels from the current layer and all the layers below (**Current & Below**) or you can sample from all the layers inside your document (**All Layers**).

There is one more option after the Sample drop-down menu worth explaining: Turn on to ignore adjustment layers when healing:

This option, when checked, allows you to sample from all layers but ignoring any adjustment layers in your document.

48 Close the image when done.

Healing Brush tool is also great when removing objects from the images. Yes, you can use Clone Stamp tool , however that Healing Brush tool will blend the content when healing. Clone Stamp tool doesn't do it.

49 Open **cafe.jpg** from the Images folder.

In this exercise, you are going to remove objects from the image. If you are following along with the image from the Images folder, then you are going to remove the text embedded in the menu on the table.

50 Zoom into **100%** view or more, focusing on the text on the menu.

This time, you are going to use a slightly different way of healing. You are not going to duplicate the background layer, instead you will create a blank new layer to work on.

51 Create a blank new layer using New Layer icon at the bottom of the Layers panel (or using Layer > New > Layer...)

52 Select Healing Brush tool.

53 In the Options bar set the size of the brush to around 15-20px and set the Hardness of the brush to around 80-90%.

54 Leave Mode on **Normal**, Source **Sampled** and check **Aligned**. Keep Sample set to **All Layers**.

55 Sample from the are next to the text with Alt/Opt key down and start painting over the text to remove it from the image as shown here:

Keep on painting until you remove all the text from the menu. Notice how the Healing Brush tool seamlessly blends the pixels so that it looks as if the text never was on the cover of the menu.

Spot Healing Brush tool

Spot Healing Brush tool, which as you may have noticed is the default retouching tool as it appears initially on the top of the stack of healing tools, is another healing tool on the group, but it works a bit different from Healing Brush tool. If you try to Alt/Opt click with the Spot Healing Brush tool, you will get this message:

Spot Healing Brush tool samples automatically from the area around the cursor. You're going to see how it works on the logo that appears above the text on the cover of the menu. Because Spot Healing Brush tools works by analysing the pixels from the surrounding area, you will need to work with layer containing pixels.

56 Select Spot Healing Brush tool and using the Options bar set the size of the brush.

57 Set the Type to **Proximity Match**.

Proximity Match type analyses pixels around the cursor and finds the best area to sample from and replace the pixels that are painted on.

Create Texture type creates a texture pattern based on the area around the cursor.

Content-Aware type will be explained in just a moment.

58 For Spot Healing Brush tool you need a layer with pixels, so duplicate the background layer first.

59 Start painting over the logo on the cover of the menu.

60 With just a few clicks the logo should be gone.

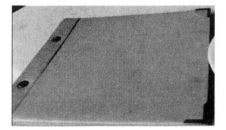

Proximity Match is great for most work with the Spot Healing Brush tool, but there may be situations when it doesn't work too well. Situations like when you brush in very contrasty sections of the image, where Proximity Match produces bleeding effect near the contrasty edge. That's where **Content-Aware** type comes in.

Content-Aware type has only been added to Photoshop recently, in version CS5. It intelligently looks into the image and works out how to blend the pixels to create the most natural effect. Let's see what you can do with Content-Aware type in the Spot Healing Brush.

61 You can close cafe image.

62 Open **malta.jpg** from the Images folder.

63 Duplicate the background layer so that you don't work on the original.

You're going to remove the electricity/telephone lines within the image that are hanging between the buildings.

64 First, try using the Proximity Match type for Spot Healing Brush tool on one of the lines.

That's what I got:

65 Now change the type to **Content-Aware** and go over the same area:

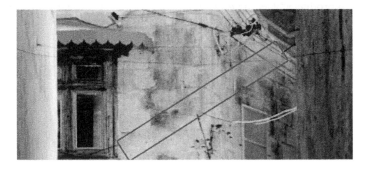

You can see a big difference between these two types, two techniques using the same tool. Content-Aware type does magic within the images. Real magic.

66 Go ahead and use the Spot Healing Brush tool with Type set to Content-Aware to remove all the lines between the buildings.

Patch Tool

Patch tool is another selection tool found in the same group as the Healing Brush and Spot Healing Brush. Because Patch tool is grouped together with Healing brush, it uses the same techniques for performing calculations. What's different about the Patch tool is that you can use this tool on bigger areas by creating 'patches'. It works like Lasso tool which we will go through later on.

One of my favourite features of the Patch tool is that it gives you a preview of what's going on when you start applying it. Patch tool needs to work with layers with pixels, so you will need to duplicate the layer with the image to start with.

As an example here, you are going to use the Patch tool to remove the cable that runs along the wall on the right side of the image. You can see the cable on the screenshot here:

67 Duplicate the layer with the image and rename it.

68 With the new layer selected, select the **Patch** tool.

69 In the Options bar, in the first set of icons leave the first icon selected (New Selection) and Patch set to **Normal** and **Source** active as shown on the screenshot here.

Note: Patch tool now has a new option under Patch - Content-Aware. More on Content-Aware in the next section.

70 Click and drag holding the mouse button down to create an outline around a part of the cable on the wall:

71 With the outline created, click inside, hold the mouse button down and drag to reposition the patch to the part of the wall above.

72 Release the mouse button.

The patch beautifully blends into the background and creates a nice soft transition between the two areas of the wall. I like thinking about the Patch tool as being like a Healing Brush tool for bigger areas as these two tools work in similar way.

73 Keep on retouching with the Patch tool until the entire cable is gone.

Note: Notice that the Patch tool keep the selection active - "marching ants" as they're called - until you click again with the Patch tool to create a new patch. You can also deselect the marching ants using **Select > Deselect** *from the application menu.*

Content-Aware Fill

Now it is time for **Content-Aware Fill** - another example of great Content-Aware technology implemented into Photoshop by Adobe engineers. Content-Aware Fill works great even though you don't have much control over how it works. All you need to do is to create a selection and apply Content-Aware Fill which will do the rest.

Content-Aware Fill is great for removing objects from images in a quick and easy way and replacing them with sampled surrounding pixels. And that's what I like about this technique most - it's quick and it's easy (and it's amazing!).

You can also use Content-Aware option with the Patch tool, but here we are going to focus on the Content-Aware Fill. You are going to remove the door in the wall on the right side of the image.

74 Still working on malta.jpg, flatten the image using **Layer > Flatten Image**.

75 Using the Lasso tool create an outline around the door including some of the wall within your outline:

76 Once you've got the selection, press **Delete** key on your keyboard.

Pressing Delete key on your keyboard will invoke the Fill dialogue box. If it does't, make sure that you're working on a background layer as this technique with the keyboard shortcut will only work on the background layer.

If you're not working on the background layer, pressing Delete key on your keyboard will delete the area that has been selected. In this case, instead of using Delete key, use Edit > Fill. This will bring the same dialogue box.

77 When the Fill dialogue box opens, from the **Use** drop-down menu choose

Content-Aware and click OK:

In just a few seconds the door in the wall should be gone. If there are any parts of the door remaining, reapply the Content-Aware:

78 Create another selection if needed and press **Delete** key again to invoke Fill dialogue box.

Here is my image after applying Content-Aware Fill:

This is one of examples of using Content-Aware Fill inside Photoshop CS6. You can keep removing the bush by the wall if you want. I've managed to remove the entire bush by the wall with just a few selections.

Content-Aware Move Tool (New in CS6)

Content-Aware Move Tool is a new addition to the family of Content-Aware technology built into Adobe Photoshop. Content-Aware Move Tool is a bit similar to the Patch tool, however it uses Content-Aware technology to intelligently move the content around.

Content-Aware Move Tool has two modes: **Move** and **Extend**:

The Mode allows you to either move an object to another location and blend it into the background or extend it.

Adaptation allows you to control how the object will be copied and blended into the background.

79 Open keyboard.jpg from the Images folder.

You are going to use this example to change keys on the keyboard. You are going to remove the arrow from one of the keys and move the delete key onto it using the Content-Aware Move tool.

80 Remove the arrow on the key on the right side of the image using one of the retouching

tools.

81 Create a blank new layer.

82 With the new layer selected, select **Content-Aware Move Tool**.

83 In the Options bar set Mode to **Move** and check **Sample All Layers**.

Note: The reason why you need to check Sample All Layers is because you are going to work on a blank layer and sample from the layer below. If you don't check Sample All Layers and you click and drag with Content-Aware Move tool, you will see this error message:

84 Create an outline around the text that reads Delete, including the Delete logo.

85 Once you've created the outline, click and drag to reposition the text and the logo to another key on the right like that:

Now the text and the logo are gone from the key on the left and are blending into the key on the right!

86 Deselect the selection by choosing **Select > Deselect**.

87 If it doesn't look straight, use **Edit > Transform > Rotate** and rotate it slightly.

88 If you got the shadowing around the text, especially on the left, use Clone Stamp tool to remove it.

Here's before and after:

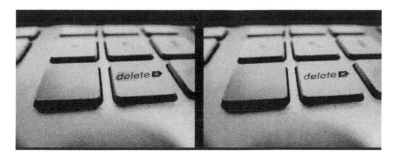

89 You can close the file.

Retouching Portraits

In this part of the lesson you need to find an image you can work on. When retouching images you need to remember to only apply minimal number of retouching techniques, unless you're going to do fashion beauty retouching. Try to keep images looking natural. Make it subtle.

If I can give you some tips on retouching, it would be these:

- Keep your brush small and zoom into the image. Retouchers work most of the time at 100% and more. The smaller your brush the more precise you can be. I often work with a very small brush, often smaller than 10px.

- I'll be mentioning it later again, but work with semi-transparent brush. Set your brush's opacity quite low. I will explain that later. You can always apply the brush strokes a few times to build up the effect.

- Invest in a Wacom tablet. Your life will be so much easier and you're going to do more work in shorter amount of time. A Wacom tablet and a pen are a must for every serious Photoshop user and all the Photoshop retouchers and artists use them.

Here's the Wacom tablet that I have been using for the last few years:

- Work on separate layers. Working on separate layers allows you to quickly edit layers, change their opacity or delete them.

- As you spend a lot of time on one image retouching it, take a break. Come back after a moment and inspect the image. The image may look good and may not need any further retouching. Avoid overdoing.

90 Open the image you want to work on.

91 Create a blank new layer for retouching.

92 If there are any skin blemishes, use the Healing Brush tool to remove them.

93 If you want to lighten the eyes, select the Brush tool, set the Brush size to very small and apply some white strokes on a separate layer with lowered Opacity of the Brush:

94 If the eyes look too white (initially they may), lower the opacity of the layer:

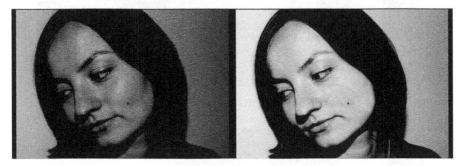

This is my before and after:

These techniques should give you an idea on how to use different retouching tools to create the desired effect and as usual - practise makes perfect!

Just before we finish, a few more words about using tools for retouching.

If you use tools with certain settings, save them as presets. Here's what you can do.

95 With the tool you are using selected, click the tool's icon in the far left of the **Options bar**.

96 When the drop-down menu appears, click the little page icon on the right side (or click on the little gear icon and choose **New Tool Preset...**:

97 Give the Preset a name and click OK.

Congratulations on successfully completing another lesson.

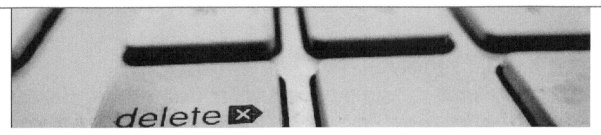

Lesson 05

Pen Tool Selections

Things you are going to learn in this lesson are:

- How the Pen tool works

- Creating Selections with the Pen tool

- Extracting Objects from Images

- Compositing Images

- Adding Vector Watermarks

Pen tool and Paths

We will be talking about selections in detail in the next chapter but for now let me just say that there is another way of creating selections and that is with the Pen tool. Aside for the ability to create selections, Pen tool is a fantastic tool that lets you create Paths. What are paths, you may be asking? Let me put it this way to get you started - Paths are great if you work with large files, they can be stored within the file and converted to selection at any time.

That's what you are going to do in this lesson - you will create a path with the Pen tool and then you will convert it into a selection. Maybe you will even save the path so that you could reuse it in the future.

Pen tool has three modes:

1. Shape mode;

2. Path mode;

3. Pixels mode.

Don't worry about the last one, you will only be using the first one or the second one. Shape mode creates a shape layer and Path mode creates a path without any colour and without creating any new layers. Unless you want to draw something you will use the Path mode.

In this part of the lesson I am going to use the image of the monitor and the Pen tool will be used to create a path around the monitor's screen so that a new image could be put inside. If you want to follow along with the same image, the image of the monitor can be downloaded from the StockXchange website: http://www.sxc.hu.

This is the image from StockXchange that I'm going to use:

1 Open the image of the monitor (or your own image).

2 Zoom into the image to see the monitor's screen closer.

3 Select the **Pen tool** from the Tools panel:

4 In the Options Bar set the mode to Path (Path is the default setting) and leave the other options for now:

5 Position your cursor in one corner of the monitor's screen and click to set an anchor point:

6 Release the mouse button, move the cursor to another corner and click again.

7 Repeat the last step in the third corner of the monitor's screen.

The last step, in the fourth corner, is going to be a bit different. I will explain that in the next step.

8 Move the cursor into the fourth corner and you should see a circle icon next to the cursor. If you the circle, click to add the final anchor point and close the path at same time.

9 Once you've created a path, you will find it in the **Paths** panel, so open it by clicking on the Paths panel tab positioned behind the Layers panel (or alternatively choose **Window > Paths**).

You should see your path here:

Paths panel overview

At the bottom of the Paths panel there is a series of icons. Here's what they do, from left to right:

Fill Path - fill the path with your current colour,

Stroke Path - stroke the path with your currently selected painting tool,

Load Path as a Selection - load your path as a selection (you're going to do it in just a moment),

Make Work Path from a Selection - convert your selection into a work path,

Add Mask - add a mask,

Create New Path - this option creates a blank new path,

Delete - delete a path.

146

Note: There is another interesting option when using Create New Path icon and we will go through it in this lesson.

Now that you have created your path, you can convert it into a selection.

10 In the Paths panel, with the Path selected, click on **Load Path as a Selection** icon.

This will convert your path into a selection like on a screenshot here:

11 Open an image that you would like to insert into the selection.

12 With the new image open, choose **Select > All** and **Edit > Copy**.

13 Now with the image in the clipboard, navigate back to the monitor image.

14 Choose **Edit > Paste Special > Paste Into**.

Now the image will appear inside the monitor:

Notice that the image appeared on its own layer:

15 Close the image you copied.

Because the image you've pasted into the monitor's screen is now on its own layer, you can easily edit it.

16 The image you've pasted may have a different aspect ratio from the monitor's screen so resize it using **Edit > Transform > Scale**.

17 Once you're done resizing, remember to accept the transformation by clicking the Accept icon in the Options bar (or by pressing Enter key on the keyboard).

18 Position the image where you want it to appear within the monitor using the **Move tool**.

Extracting Objects with Pen tool

Now that you have created a simple path and even turned it into a selection, wouldn't it be nice if you could create more complex paths? What about shapes that are not squares or rectangles? That's what you're going to do now. You will use the Pen tool to create more complex selection and you will extract the object from the background.

19 Keep the monitor image open. You will need it again in just a moment.

20 Open **iconia.jpg** from Images folder (or your own image).

In this exercise, you're going to create a path around the usb port on the side of the tablet, make it into a selection, and duplicate it on the right side of the tablet.

21 Select the Pen tool if you don't have it already selected.

22 Make sure that in the Options bar you have your Pen tool selected so it creates a **Path**.

23 Position the first anchor point on the edge of the usb port:

24 Click at the end of the straight line at the top to set another anchor point.

25 Now position the cursor at the beginning of the straight vertical line after the corner:

26 Click, hold the mouse button down, and start dragging mouse downwards to create a curve.

27 Release the mouse button when the curve aligns with the edge of the port:

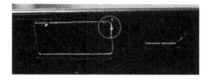

28 Before you create straight line, you will need to remove one out of two handles that now appeared (they will appear every time you create a curve with Pen tool).

29 Hold down Alt/Opt key and click on the anchor point you have just created.

One of the handles will now be gone so that you can go ahead and create additional anchor points.

30 Move the cursor to the end of the straight line and click to set an anchor point:

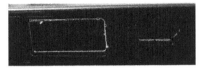

31 Repeat Step 25 to 27 to create path around another corner.

32 Repeat Step 28 to 29 to remove one of the handles.

33 Keep going around until the entire usb port is selected with a path.

Here's what the path should look like. Don't worry if you don't get it perfect as I will show you how to edit your path.

Once you've finished the path, it's time to edit it. For editing the path you will be using **Direct Selection tool**:

34 With Direct Selection tool selected click anywhere on the path.

When you click on the path with Direct Selection tool, the entire path gets selected and you can see all the anchor points that were created with Pen tool. Now you can use the tool to edit the path. This is the beauty of using the Pen tool for creating paths/selections, you have total control over the path.

35 Click and drag on any of the anchor points that you want to reposition.

36 If you want to change the curve, click on the anchor point and the curve and the handle will appear as shown here on the screenshot:

37 Keep refining the path until you are happy with the outline.

Note: If you want to be really precise adjusting the position of the anchor points, click the anchor point with Direct Selection tool and use the arrow keys on your keyboard to reposition them 1 pixel at a time. To move them faster hold Shift key down as you're using the arrow keys.

38 When done load the path as a selection using the icon at the bottom of the Paths panel.

39 Select **Move tool**.

40 Hold **Alt/Opt** key on the keyboard and drag the selection to a new location.

41 Position the selected area on the right side of the image, and release the mouse button.

Next release **Alt/Opt** key.

42 Once the object is placed, choose **Edit > Cut**.

43 Choose **Layer > New > Layer...** and give it a name.

44 With new layer selected choose **Edit > Paste Special > Paste in Place**.

Now you've got the selected area (in my case a usb port) in the same location, but on its own layer. Because the object now resides on its own layer, it is easy to reposition or resize.

Rubber Band mode

As you were looking through the options for Pen tool, you may have noticed an option called Rubber Band:

Rubber Band mode, when ticked, will display the outline of the path as you're drawing it, which some people find distracting. It is a very useful feature, though. It allows you to see how your path is being created (a bit like using Lasso tool, which we will use later when we explore selections). What makes Rubber Band mode different from the 'normal' Pen tool is that you don't need to wait for a click to see the outline of the path you are working on.

45 The object on a new layer (in my case a usb port) may need some repositioning or rotating. Use **Edit > Transform > Rotate** to rotate it or **Edit > Transform > Scale** to make it smaller if needed.

46 If you're scaling the image remember to hold **Shift** key down or click the chain icon in the Options bar so that Photoshop doesn't distort it.

Note: Remember when using Transform, when done you will need to click on the Accept or Cancel icon in the Options bar before moving on.

Adding Vector Watermarks

In this section of the chapter you are going to add a watermark to the image or design. And you're going to do it using vector tools in Photoshop to give you flexibility of the object that can be scaled up and down without loosing the quality.

Shape tools in Photoshop CS6 are now vector tools. Great new for graphic designers. And you are going to use that for a watermark on an image.

Copyrighting your images got so tricky nowadays with almost all websites on the web designed in HTML because anyone can easily download your images either by right-clicking on them and choosing Download or Save.. or by clicking and dragging your image to their desktop.

Note: If you want to find out more on ways to protect your images from being downloaded and used, have a look at a post I created on my blog at PhotoshopLightroomBridge.co.uk.

Here's a link for you:

http://bit.ly/XqiwzD

47 Open the image you want to work on.

I'm going to work on the image of the monitor we were working on earlier.

48 Once the image is opened, select the top layer in the layers panel.

You need to create the watermark above all the layers so that it will appear in front of everything else.

49 With the top layer selected click on **Custom Shape tool**:

50 With Custom Shape tool selected navigate to the Options Bar and set Tool Mode to

Shape, set **Fill** and **Stroke**:

In **Photoshop CC**, there is a slight change to the Stroke in the Options bar:

51 Click on the **Shape** drop-down menu in the Options bar and you'll a list of shapes

available:

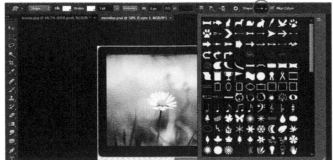

If you don't see that many shapes, you will need to load them. The next few steps will show you how.

52 Click on the Shape drop-down menu to reveal the icons of the shapes.

53 Click the gear icon in the top right corner, which will reveal menu like this:

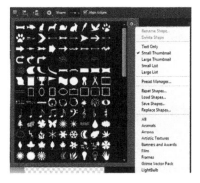

54 From the menu choose **All**.

55 In the dialogue box that appears click OK to replace all existing shapes or Append to add new shapes at the bottom:

If you're starting from fresh and you haven't loaded any shapes yet, click OK.

56 Now you'll see all shapes available with Photoshop. Scroll down the list and find the copyright symbol. Double-click on it to select it.

57 Click, hold the Shift key down and start dragging to create the copyright symbol on the image.

58 Release the mouse button when you're happy with the size of the symbol. Then release the Shift key.

Note: The reason why you hold down the Shift key is to constrain the proportions of the image so as to create a perfect circular copyright shape, not a distorted one.

59 Use Move tool to reposition the shape.

Now you're going to position the copyright symbol so that it is exactly in the centre of the monitor (horizontally). Aligning objects in Photoshop is done with Move tool. There is no Align panel in Photoshop.

60 Make sure you have Move tool selected.

61 Click on the shape layer in the layers panel to select it.

62 Hold **Ctrl** (Win) or **Cmd** (Mac) and click on the bottom layer (the layer with the monitor) to select both layers (shape and monitor).

63 In the Options bar click **Align Horizontal Centers** icon:

Now the copyright symbol is exactly in the centre of the monitor.

64 Position the copyright symbol vertically.

65 Navigate to the Layers panel and select just the shape layer.

You are now going to change the shape to make it transparent with just the outline and a bevel effect showing through.

66 Click on **Fx** icon at the bottom of the Layers panel and from the drop-down menu

choose **Bevel & Emboss...**

67 When the **Layer Style** dialogue box opens, just click OK for now.

68 In the Layers panel set **Fill** of the layer to **0%**:

Now that you've set the Fill of the layer to 0%, you can see the effect. It is time to start editing the Bevel & Emboss effect. And that's what you're going to do now.

69 Double-click on the Bevel & Emboss layer effect in the Layers panel to edit it.

70 Experiment with different **Styles**:

71 Once you've chosen the Style, look through **Techniques**:

72 Finally tweak the settings for **Size** and/or **Soften** if required.

Congratulations! You have successfully finished this lesson and you should now have a beautiful semi-transparent watermark on your image. This is the effect we were after:

Lesson 06

Selections

Things you are going to learn in this lesson are primarily selection tools like:

- Rectangular Marquee tool

- Elliptical Marquee tool

- Magic Wand tool

- Quick Selection tool

- Lasso, Polygonal Lasso and Magnetic Lasso tools

- Saving and Editing Selections

- Refine Edge

Selections

Mastering Photoshop requires you to have skills in many different areas. When editing and enhancing images, you will need another very important skill and that is creating selections. If you don't create a selection, any changes you make to the image will apply to the entire image. Selections are a way of telling Photoshop which areas of the image you want to apply the effect to and which areas you want to leave untouched.

Selections are such an important aspect of working with Photoshop documents and mastering selections is a highly valued skill. There are many ways of controlling selections and many selection tools. That's why we are going to cover all different selection tools and explain how they work. This will give you knowledge of different selection tools and you will be able to choose the best tool for what you are going to do.

Rectangular Marquee tool

Rectangular Marquee tool lets you create selections that are squares or rectangles. Rectangular Marquee tool is a great tool for creating quick selections that are blocks with regular shapes. It's best if you try it on an example. You're going to work with an image of a rectangular red bar and you will make the image into an English flag with the red cross (St. George's cross).

1 Open the **red_bar.png** image from the images folder.

2 Set the zoom to 100% using **View > Actual Pixels**.

3 Select the **Rectangular Marquee tool** from the Tools panel:

4 Position the cursor in the top left corner of the red bar, click, hold the mouse button down and start dragging until you get to the bottom right corner of the red bar. Then release.

Your selection will look like this:

Note: As you're holding the mouse button down and dragging, press and hold the Spacebar. This will access the Move tool temporarily and you will be able to reposition the marquee before you release the mouse button. Just remember, as you're holding the Spacebar, hold the mouse button down all the time, and release the mouse button after releasing the Spacebar.

5 As your selection is still running (the selection you see if often called "marching ants"), you can still use the Arrow keys on your keyboard to reposition the selection.

6 Copy your selection onto a new layer using **Layer > New > Layer Via Copy**.

Layer Via Copy command copies your existing selection onto a new layer leaving the content on the original layer as well. You will be using this command a lot, preserving the original background layer. It's worth remembering the keyboard shortcut Ctrl/Cmd+J.

7 Your selection disappears and a new layer with the red bar appears in the Layers panel:

8 Double-click on the name of the new layer to rename it. Name it **Horizontal Bar**.

9 Now that you have the horizontal bar on its own layer, duplicate it by dragging the layer onto the New Layer icon at the bottom of the Layers panel.

Note: Remember that if you prefer using menu, you can use Layer > Duplicate Layer...

10 Rename the new layer to **Vertical Bar**.

Now that you've got two layers that look the same, you are going to rotate the Vertical Bar layer to make it vertical so that the image will have a cross. Then, you will change the background behind the cross as the English flag has a white background.

11 With the Vertical Bar layer selected, choose **Edit > Transform > Rotate 90° CW**.

Now you get a beautiful and evenly spaced red cross in the centre of the image. By the way, it doesn't matter whether you have rotated the image clockwise (CW) or counter-clockwise (CCW). It will still look the same.

Now it's time to do something with the background. If it's supposed to be the English flag, it needs a white background. As usual, I will encourage you to keep the original background, so you're going to create a new layer above the background.

12 Select the Background layer and create a new layer above it.

You can either click on New Layer icon at the bottom of the Layers panel or you can choose **Layer > New > Layer...**.

13 Rename new layer to **White Background**.

14 Fill the new layer using **Edit > Fill**.

15 When **Fill** dialogue box opens, choose White from **Use** drop-down menu:

16 Save the file as you will need it later on. Save it as either PSD or TIFF to save the document with all the layers.

Elliptical Marquee tool

Elliptical Marquee tool is very similar to Rectangular Marquee tool as it works in a very similar way. With one exception. It creates selections that have elliptical or oval shapes.

The example you are going to work on here is an example of extracting wheels from the image of a car.

17 Open **ibiza.jpg**.

18 Zoom in very close to the front wheel.

19 Select **Elliptical Marquee** tool:

20 Position the cursor in the top left corner of the wheel, click and start dragging.

21 If you need to reposition the selection before you release the mouse button, hold the Spacebar down.

22 Once you've got the wheel selected (just the alloys), release the mouse button.

23 Copy the selection onto a new layer.

24 Name the layer **Front Wheel**.

25 Repeat the steps to select the rear wheel (just remember to select the Background layer) and name the layer **Rear Wheel**.

By now, you should have wheels on separate layers, like on the screenshot here (the wheels on the layers' thumbnails highlighted in circles):

26 Save the document as you may need it later on.

27 Close the document.

Magic Wand tool

Magic Wand tool is one of the oldest selection tools in Photoshop. Unlike Marquee tools, Magic Wand tool doesn't create selections based on shapes. One could say that it creates irregular selections. What is specific to Magic Wand is that it creates selection based on **colour**. Many people often get frustrated with Magic Wand and call it "Tragic Wand" (the name became quite popular), but once you understand how it works, you will see that it is actually a very useful selection tool that works great in certain situations.

Let's start with simple example so that you can see how Magic Wand tool works.

28 Reopen the image with the English flag you have earlier created, if you closed it.

29 Hide all the layers except the Background layer by clicking on layers' eye icons to turn their visibility off:

30 Make the Background layer your active layer by clicking on it.

31 Select **Magic Wand** tool:

32 In the Options Bar, in the first series of icons, click the first one - New Selection:

Let's have a look at the options for Magic Wand tool.

The options from left:

- the first set of icons (4 of them) - **New Selection, Add to Selection, Subtract from Selection, Intersect with Selection**. These icons allow you to decide if you want to start creating a new selection or maybe add or subtract from an existing one.

- **Sample Size** - you can choose if you want to sample from just one pixel or a bigger area. A common setting for Sample Size used is **5 by 5 Average**.

- **Tolerance** - it sets how different in tone and colour a pixel can be from the area you click on, e.g. if you set the Tolerance to 20 and click on area that is very light grey, Photoshop will select all the pixels that are up to 20 levels darker and brighter shades of this colour.

Let's give it a try before we move on.

33 With **New Selection** icon selected set **Tolerance** to **20** and click in the middle of the grey background:

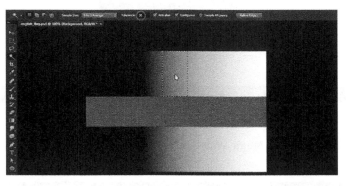

What Photoshop did here was selecting all pixels that are up to 20 levels darker and brighter from the area you clicked on.

Note: Don't worry if you have bottom part of the image selected as well. I will explain in just a moment.

34 Remove the selection by choosing **Select > Deselect**.

35 Change the **Tolerance** to **100** and click in the same area within the image:

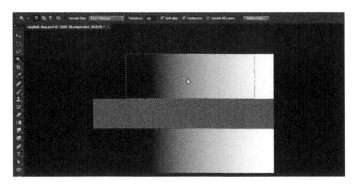

Notice the difference between these two settings for Tolerance. That's how it works. The higher the Tolerance setting the wider the range of selection.

Back to the **Options** bar, moving to the right:

Anti-Alias - since Magic Wand selects pixels within the image and pixels are square, selection may often appear jagged. That's where Anti-Alias comes in. Anti-aliasing is smoothing the edges by applying a small blur to them. By default, anti-aliasing is turned on and we'll leave it like that.

Contiguous - did you notice how when I clicked in the area above the gradient, Photoshop would only select the pixels above the gradient in both situations? The reason for that is the **Contiguous** - with Contiguous selected, Photoshop will only select pixels that are side by side within the same area.

Sample All Layers - by default, when you click on the image, Photoshop only selects pixels on the active layer. If you work with a document with multiple layers, you may want to include pixels from other layers in your selection. That's what Sample All Layers option is for.

Let's see what the selection will look like with Contiguous unchecked and then we'll move on to the next image.

36 Back to our image, if you uncheck **Contiguous** and click on the grey area within the image, Photoshop will select all grey pixels in the image:

37 You can close the image and don't need to save it.

38 Open **ibiza.psd** or **ibiza.tiff** depending what you saved it as.

39 Select **Magic Wand** tool, click **New Selection** icon and set Opacity to around **50**.

Check **Contiguous**.

40 Make **Background** layer the active layer.

41 Click on the sky to select it:

Almost the entire sky got selected. You just need to refine the selection. It looks like you need a higher value for Tolerance.

42 Deselect the selection by choosing **Select > Deselect**.

43 Increase the Tolerance to **60**.

44 Click in the sky again.

Now the selection should look much better. The entire sky should be selected, like on the screenshot here:

Now that you've managed to create a selection of the sky, you are going to inverse the selection to select the foreground instead of the sky and copy it onto a new layer.

45 With the selection running choose **Select > Inverse**.

Now the foreground will be selected instead of the sky. You have just inversed the selection.

46 With the background layer selected choose **Layer > New > Layer Via Copy** or press **Ctrl+J/Cmd+J**.

47 Rename new layer to **Foreground**.

48 Select the background layer and apply Levels adjustment layer using the Adjustments panel.

49 Darken the sky using the Levels adjustment:

50 Save the file as you may need it later and close it.

And that's how Magic Wand tool works. It's a great tool when working with areas within the image that are of the same or similar colour. In many situations you will need some more sophisticated selection tools as you will be working with very complicated backgrounds.

One of the examples where Magic Wand tool comes in handy that I can think of are situations when you work with images that were taken in a studio as these images will have plain backgrounds and it will be easy to select them with Magic Wand.

Now to another tool that will also allow you to select parts of the image based on colour but with some additional features.

Quick Selection tool

Quick Selection tool works in a similar way to Magic Wand tool in a way that is also creates selections based on colour. But when it's different from Magic Wand is that it also works like a brush. This makes it one of my favourite selection tools in Photoshop. I use Quick Selection tool quite a lot. I often find it to be a great selection tool to start with, to create an initial selection, and then refine the selection with another tool.

Let's see how it works in practise. You are going to select and extract a person from the background using Quick Selection tool. Or actually, youa re going to select and extract a person in a costume (just a joke).

51 Open **malta_2.jpg**:

As you can see, in this example, even though it looks like the costume on the person is grey, there are so many different shades of grey so you wouldn't use Magic Wand tool. It looks like a perfect job for my favourite - Quick Selection tool.

I will take you step-by-step to show you how to make Quick Selection tool work for you and work the way you want it to work. I often hear from people who haven't used Quick Selection tool before that it's so hard to master it. Let me show you that it's not.

52 Select **Quick Selection** tool:

53 Zoom into the image (around 100% will be fine).

54 In the Options bar click on the drop-down menu next to the number with the size:

55 In this drop-down menu you can choose the size of the brush. Keep it quite small. I used **20** pixels here.

56 Leave the Hardness set to **100%**.

57 Click away within the Options bar to close the drop-down menu.

58 Make sure that **Auto-Enhance** is checked.

Note: Auto-Enhance will make a big difference to your selections. As you move your cursor around the object you want to select, Auto-Enhance will expand the selection to the edges of the object. It's an absolutely amazing feature!

59 Don't worry about **Sample All Layers** option. This document only has one layer.

60 Finally make sure that in the row of Quick Selection icons, at the left side of the Options bar, the first one (without plus or minus) is selected as shown here:

61 Position the cursor over the person in the image (the bear), click and start slowly dragging your cursor around:

62 Keep the cursor away from the edges and just slowly move it around expanding your selection until you get the entire bear:

Don't worry if you're selecting some background. For now just focus on selecting the entire object.

63 Once you've done the initial selection, use the icons with plus (+) or minus (-) in the Options bar to add or subtract from your selection:

In my situation I have selected some of the background on the right side of the bear:

64 In this case I will use Subtract from Selection option from the Options bar (-) and will slowly paint over the area that needs to be removed from the selection.

*Note: You can add to your existing selection by holding down **Shift key** and subtract from your existing selection by holding down **Alt key**.*

65 Once you've refined your selection, copy the bear onto a new layer using **Layer > New > Layer Via Copy**.

You've successfully created selection using another selection tool. It is time for another tool.

66 You can close the image.

Lasso and Polygonal Lasso tools

Lasso tools come in three versions: Lasso tool, Polygonal Lasso tool, and Magnetic Lasso tool.

- **Lasso** tool creates freehand selections (you may need a steady hand for that and a Wacom tablet will help).

- **Polygonal Lasso** tool creates straight lines, which makes it great for selecting objects with straight lines like a door or a window.

- **Magnetic Lasso** tool auto-detects the edges between the contrasty pixels. This one is the most useful of the Lasso tools and one of the most often used selection tools in Photoshop.

Let's start with the first two lasso tools so that you can get some practise on how they work. You are going to extract a window from an image.

67 Open blue_window.jpg from the images folder.

68 Zoom into the image, but not too close. Make sure you can see the entire window.

69 Select **Lasso** tool:

70 In the Options bar make sure that the icon for a new selection is selected:

71 Position the cursor on the edge of the window, click, hold the mouse button down, and start dragging the cursor around the edge of the window:

72 Remember to hold mouse button down until you go all the way around the window and come back to where you started. Then, you can release the mouse button to close selection.

As you can see it's pretty difficult selecting objects with the Lasso tool. Even if you use a graphics tablet, your selection may not look the way you would want it. Here's mine:

73 If you like what you've done, you can copy the selection onto a new layer. Otherwise, remove the selection using **Select > Deselect**.

74 Select **Polygonal Lasso** tool.

75 In the Options bar select **New Selection** icon if it's not already selected.

76 Click in one of the corners of the window and release the mouse button.

77 Move the cursor to the end of straight line (notice how the line appears):

78 Click at the end of straight line to set an anchor point.

79 Release the mouse button, move the cursor to the end of the next straight line and click.

80 Repeat the steps for the other straight lines within the image.

81 Once you go all the way around and come back to where you started, you will notice a little circle icon next to your cursor. When you see it, click to close the selection.

Now your selection should look much better than the one you have created with Lasso tool.

You're going to move the selection of the window into a new document with transparent background. But first, I will show you another selection tool. Then, you can decide which tool will work best in this situation. Polygonal Lasso tool did a really good job here, but I have a feeling that the next tool - Magnetic Lasso tool could even do a better job. Let's give it a try.

Before you use Magnetic Lasso tool, I will show you how to save the selection you have created.

Saving Selections

You will be spending a lot of time creating selections in Photoshop. You may be selecting different parts of the image you are working on and there may be times when you would want to save all these different selections separately and reuse them in future projects. If you spend quite a bit of time working on a selection and if you plan on reusing the image in the future, you may want to save what you have done and saving selections in Photoshop is straightforward.

Selections are stored as alpha channels and they can be found in the Channels panel.

82 With your selection running choose **Select > Save Selection...**:

83 In **Save Selection** dialogue box that opens give your selection a name:

84 Click OK to save the selection.

85 Now you can deselect the selection using **Select > Deselect**.

So how do I load the selection when I need it, you may be thinking? You will find out in just a moment after you create a new selection with Magnetic Lasso tool.

Magnetic Lasso tool

You already know how the Magnetic Lasso tool works. At least theoretically. Now you will put it into practise. You are going to love this tool, it is fantastic! Again, I will guide you through step by step as once you get your head around the tool, you will be able to use it effectively.

86 Select **Magnetic Lasso** tool:

87 In the Options Bar, make sure that New Selection icon is selected.

88 Leave the other settings on their defaults.

Let me explain the options found in the Options bar for **Magnetic Lasso** tool.

Note: The options in the Options bar need to be set up before you use the tool. You cannot change them while you're moving around the edges of the object. If you want to change one of the options, once you've changed it you will need to use the Magnetic Lasso tool again to create a selection.

TIP: You can adjust the size of the Width while working on a selection by pressing the bracket keys on the keyboard - left bracket ([ ) to make it smaller and right bracket ( ]) to make it bigger.

Width - this is the area which Photoshop uses when looking at the edges. As an example, with a setting of 10 px you can move the cursor up to 10 px away from the edge and Photoshop will still select the edge. Use lower values for objects with less defined edges.

Contrast - this option determines how much difference there has to in brightness values and colour between the object you are selecting and the background so that Photoshop will see it as an edge.

TIP: You can change the Contrast setting as you are working on the selection by pressing keyboard shortcuts - comma key (,) to decrease the contrast and full stop key (.) to increase the contrast.

Frequency - as you move around the object selecting it, Photoshop creates anchor points (tiny squares) along the selection. Frequency defines how often will Photoshop place the anchor points. if you work with an image with little contrast between the object and the background, you may want to increase the frequency.

TIP: Keep the frequency on the default and if you need an anchor point, you can just click on the edge of the object to create an anchor point yourself.

89 With this tool use **View > Fit on Screen** so that the scrollbars on the sides of the image disappear.

Note: Using Fit on Screen with Magnetic Lasso tool proves to be a great solution because if you can see the scrollbars and if you move the cursor close to the edge of the image, the image will start scrolling automatically and may even disappear.

90 Position your cursor anywhere on the edge of the object.

91 Click, release the mouse button, and start slowly dragging the cursor around the edge of the window:

92 Just slowly keep moving the cursor around the window.

Note: If Photoshop places the anchor point not where you want it, you can remove it by pressing Delete key on your keyboard. If you want to remove more than one anchor point, move the cursor close to the anchor point as you're pressing Delete key because as you start moving the cursor, Photoshop will start adding new anchor points.

93 Don't worry too much if you don't get the selection right. For now go all the way around the window.

94 When you get back to where you started and when you see the circle next to your cursor, click to close the selection.

Note: If you cannot find the beginning of your selection, you can always double-click to close the selection wherever you are.

95 Now you should see "marching ants" representing your selection.

It's time to copy the selection onto a new layer, and then to load the previous selection and copy it onto a new layer as well to compare both methods of creating selections.

96 With the selection running choose **Layer > New > Layer Via Copy**.

97 Rename the new layer to **Magnetic Lasso**.

98 Select the background layer.

99 Load the previous selection (the one you've created with Polygonal Lasso tool) by choosing **Select > Load Selection…**

100 Select your selection from the **Channel** drop-down menu:

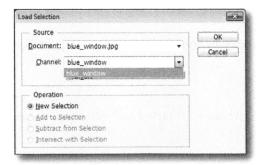

101 Click OK to load the selection.

102 Copy the selection onto a new layer can name it **Polygonal Lasso**.

Now it's time to see what both selections look like and make any necessary adjustments.

103 Hide the background layer by clicking on the eye icon next to the layers thumbnail:

104 Expand the canvas to **1200 px** Width by choosing **Image > Canvas Size...** and set the Anchor to the left:

105 Click OK to accept canvas extension.

106 Using **Move tool** reposition one of the layers to the side so that you can see both layers side by side like that:

107 Inspect both layers in detail to see which one has a better outline around the window.

By now you may be saying: "But what are these icons in the Options bar for Add, Subtract, and Intersect?". That's what we 're going to go through next. And this will be the last part of this lesson.

108 Keep the image open for the next part of the lesson.

Editing Selections

By now you know how to create selections using a number of selection tools. But what if you want to edit a selection? What if you missed something when creating a selection or what if you selected too much? That's what we are going to cover in this section of the lesson.

109 Back to the image of the window hide all the layers and reveal the background layer:

110 Create a quick selection of the window using your selection tool of choice. Don't worry about being precise.

111 With the selection running check which areas of the image you missed, I missed this:

112 No matter with selection tool you used, select **Magnetic Lasso** tool and in the
Options bar choose **Add to Selection** option:

113 Click, hold the mouse button down and start dragging around the area you missed:

114 When you go all the way around and back to where you started, when you see the circle
next to your cursor, click to close the selection.

115 Repeat the same steps for all the areas you have missed.

116 If you selected some of the background, use **Subtract from Selection** icon in the
Options bar and repeat the steps to subtract background from your selection.

117 Keep the selection running. There is one more step and it's called **Refine Edge**.

Refine Edge

Refine Edge lets you improve the edges of your selection, allowing you to extract the objects easily. I will explain the options with the steps.

118 With your selection running click **Refine Edge** button in the Options bar:

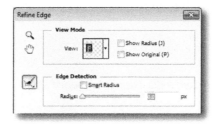

*Note: You can also choose **Select > Refine Edge...** from the menu.*

119 Here are the options in the top section of **Refine Edge**:

View Mode - use it to change how the selection is being displayed. Here are available options:

Show Radius - it displays the selection border where edge refinement happens.

Show Original - it displays the original selection.

120 Set View to **On Layers** and leave Show Radius and Show Original unchecked.

The other options in the top section of the dialogue box are:

Refine Radius tool and **Erase Refinements tool** - they allow you to precisely adjust the border of the selection.

Note: You can cycle between these two tools using a keyboard shortcut - Shift+E.

Smart Radius - it adjusts the radius for soft and hard edges near the border.

Radius - it determines the size of the border. Use small radius for sharp edges and large radius for soft edges.

121 We'll leave these two tools for now and will move to the next section - **Adjust Edge**:

Adjust Edge options:

Smooth - it creates smoother outline of the border.

Feather - it blurs the transition between the selection and the background.

Contrast - it increases the contrast on the border.

Note: Smart Radius option is more effective than the Contrast slider.

Shift Edge - it moves the border inwards or outwards thus contracting or expanding selection.

122 Play with the settings in Refine Edge dialogue box to fine tune your selection.

123 Finally, the last step is the **Output** section:

Decontaminate Colors - colour fringes are replaced with the colour of selected pixels nearby.

Output To - refined selection can become a selection or a mask on the current layer, on a new layer, or even in a new document:

124 Choose the best option that would suit you.

If you plan reusing this image and the selection you made, output the selection to a New Layer with Layer Mask. That's what I often use - **New Layer with Layer Mask**:

125 Close the document and save it when done.

126 Congratulations! You have successfully finished another lesson.

Lesson 07

Layers

Things you are going to learn in this lesson are things like:

- Layer Basics

- Layers Panel

- Layer Styles

- Transforming Layers

- Colourising Images with Adjustment Layers

- Duplicating Layers

- Grouping Layers

Layer Basics

As you have noticed already, layers are an essential element of your workflow in Photoshop. No matter what you do in Photoshop, can you imagine not being able to separate content onto separate layers? What if you want to edit one of the elements? Without layers this would be an impossible task. Layers also give you the ability to import images into Photoshop onto separate layers.

"Is there a limit to how many layers one can add in Photoshop?" I'm often asked. Well, not really. Although, there is a limit, but it's so big that you will never reach it - it's 8000 layers.

In the next exercise, you are going to create a poster for a photographic manufacturer advertising their camera. Here's a photo I took of the advert I saw in a magazine the other day:

1 Start by creating a blank new document using **File > New** (or **Ctrl+N/Cmd+N**).

2 In the New Document dialogue box choose **International Paper** from the Preset drop-down menu and then **A4** from the Size drop-down menu:

3 Leave all the rest on the defaults. Make sure that **Color Mode** is set to **RGB Color**.

4 With **Background Contents** leave it as **White** for now. Click **OK**.

Your Layers panel will display one layer called Background.

Background Layer

Background layer is always locked by default. An image can only have one background layer and the background layer cannot be repositioned meaning you cannot change the stacking order of the background layer. You cannot change its opacity or blend mode. You can convert a background layer into a normal layer and then change its opacity or blend mode (more on blend modes and opacity later). You can also convert a normal layer to a background layer (more on that later as well).

Layers Panel

Icons at the bottom of the panel (from left to right):

Link Layers, Add a Layer Style, Add layer mask, Create new fill or adjustment layer, Create a new group, Create a new layer, Delete layer.

I will explain these icons as we progress through the lessons.

Layers panel, like all panels in Photoshop, also has a menu in the top right corner:

The options from the bottom of the Layers panel can be found in this pop-up menu as well.

Let's start bringing some images and changing the background. Start with the background. The advert you are working on has a gradient in the background. You're going to add a gradient on a separate layer.

5 Create a new layer by clicking New Layer icon or choosing **Layer > New > Layer...**

6 Rename the new layer to **Gradient**.

7 Select **Gradient** tool from the Tools panel:

8 In the Options bar set the gradient to Black & White (third icon from the left):

9 From the next set of icons, choose the second one for a **Radial Gradient**:

10 Next, leave Mode as **Normal** and Opacity at **100%**.

11 If your gradient is Black to White (like mine on the previous screenshot), check **Reverse** at the far right in the Options bar.

12 With Gradient tool selected, click and drag from the top right corner of the image to the bottom left corner:

13 You can lock this layer using the lock icon above the layers in the Layers panel:

For the next steps, you will start from the top of the design and move downwards. So, next you have the Fuji logo with the green rectangle filled with a gradient.

14 Create a new layer and name it **Green gradient**.

15 Select **Polygonal Lasso** tool and draw a rectangle like this:

16 Click on the colour swatch for **Foreground** colour at the bottom of the Tools panel:

205

17 This opens **Color Picker**:

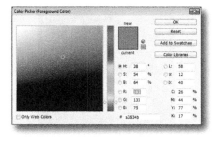

18 Inside the Color Picker choose a light green colour by clicking on the green colour in the vertical bar in the centre first, and then by clicking near the top of the big rectangle on the left:

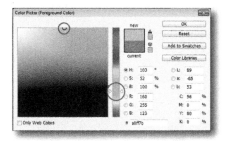

19 Click **OK.**

20 Click on the colour swatch for **Background** colour at the bottom of the Tools panel.

21 Follow the steps to change the background colour. Set it to dark green.

22 Select the Gradient tool and set the gradient to the first one - **Foreground to Background**.

23 Next, from the series of icons choose the fourth one - **Reflected Gradient**.

24 Finally, uncheck **Reverse**.

25 Click and drag at an angle inside the shape you have created in the top left corner:

Your gradient should look more or less like this one:

26 Remove the selection by choosing **Select > Deselect**.

27 You can lock the layer if you want to.

28 Save your document.

Layer Styles

Photoshop's **Layer Styles** are very popular and they're used for adding effects like drop-shadows. **Layer Styles** are non-destructive. With just a little bit of experience with layer styles you can achieve amazing results.

Adobe introduced layer styles long time ago, before Creative Suite came out, in version 6. They're very easy-to-add and customise, and Photoshop provides an easy to understand dialogue box with sliders and drop-down menus.

There are two ways of applying layer styles:

• **Presets** - found in the Styles panel,

• **Layers Styles** dialogue box.

We'll look at both, however with the Styles panel we'll just use it once so that you know how to use this feature. You'll be focusing on working with the Layer Styles dialogue box so that you could adjust the layer style the way you want it.

29 With Green gradient layer selected, choose **Window > Styles** to display Styles panel.

Styles panel allows you to quickly apply a layer style preset by simply clicking on one of the presets inside the panel. As you move the cursor over the icons the names of the styles appear as well.

30 Click on **Basic Drop Shadow** preset (or any preset you like):

It looks quite nice, doesn't it? It does, but you didn't get any dialogue box to adjust the settings. Maybe the shadow is too close or too far from the object. That's where the Layer Styles dialogue box comes in.

Notice how a new 'sub-layer', as we could call it, appears in the Layers panel:

This is your layer style. Now that it appears in the Layers panel, you can edit it.

One of the big advantages of using layer styles is that not only they are non-destructive, but they're also fully editable. You can edit them any time you want.

31 In the Layers panel double-click on the name of the layer style.

32 Layer Styles dialogue box opens:

The name of the layer styles that was used will be highlighted and checked on the left side of the dialogue box.

33 Adjust the settings for the effect by adjusting the Distance and Size, maybe Angle as well. I used Distance of **11** and Size of **20**.

34 Click **OK** when done.

Let me explain to you some options that are available in the Layer Style dialogue box next.

Layer Style dialogue box explained:

On the left there is a list of available layer styles. Each layer style has its own set of options, specific to this layer style. To apply the layer style, make sure that the layer style you want to apply is checked in the box next to the name and its name is highlighted.

Multiple layer styles can be stacked, one on top of another.

35 Now find a logo that you could use on the shape you have just created (make sure it has transparent background) and open it.

36 With the logo open, change the arrangement of the documents so that you can see both at the same time (**Window > Arrange > 2-up Vertical**).

37 Select Move tool, click on the logo, hold the mouse button down and drag it into the poster.

You should now have logo inside your poster:

38 Scale the logo down if needed, using **Edit > Transform > Scale**.

Note: remember to hold Shift key down as you're scaling the image so that you don't distort it.

39 Position the logo on top of the shape you have created.

40 Rename the layer.

41 Select Text (Horizontal Type) tool:

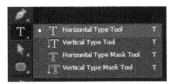

Now you're going to add some text, the name of the camera, in the top right corner of the advert. The first step will be to select an appropriate font.

42 In the Options bar choose an appropriate font from the Font Family drop-down menu:

43 Set the Font Size and then set the text alignment to **Right align text**:

Note: You can change the font properties like font family and font size later on.

44 Set the colour for your text using the colour picker in the Options bar (the icon on the right side of the text alignment icons).

45 With the text options set up click in the top right corner of the page and type the name of the camera. I typed **FINEPIX F600 EXR** and used font family **Impact**:

46 Once you've typed the text, click the tick in the Options bar to accept the text:

47 Add a **Drop Shadow** effect to the text layer to give it more depth.

48 Once you've added a Drop Shadow, change the colour of the text to **white**:

Note: If you're wondering how to change the colour of the text once you've typed the text, here's how:

1. *Select the layer with the text*

2. *Select Text tool*

3. *In the Options bar click the colour swatch and change the colour.*

Moving down the design, now you're going to draw a circle and type text inside it. The text inside the circle will then be rotated to put it at certain angle.

49 Select **Ellipse** tool:

50 In the Options bar set Pick tool mode to **Shape** and set the Fill colour and Stroke to **red**:

51 Position the cursor below the text in the top right corner of the design, click and start dragging to draw a circle. Hold the **Shift** key as you drag.

Note: Holding Shift key down as you drag with the Ellipse tool will create a perfect circle.

Note: If you hold Spacebar as you drag you can reposition the object (remember to hold the mouse button down all the time).

52 When the circle reaches the size you want release the mouse button first and then the Shift key next.

53 If you need to reposition the circle use Move tool.

54 Select Text tool again (Horizontal Type tool), click and type **Exclusive to FOTOSHOP**.

55 Accept the text by clicking the tick icon and set text alignment to Center. Resize text if needed and position it inside the circle:

Now it's time to rotate the text inside the circle.

56 With text layer selected choose **Edit > Transform > Rotate**.

57 Rotate the text like that:

58 Accept the rotation by clicking the tick icon in the Options bar.

Now it's time to bring in the image of the camera. You can use your own image or something you purchased or downloaded from one of the online libraries. I'm going to use this image of Fuji camera:

59 Place the image of the camera directly into the design by choosing **File > Place...**

60 Select the image and place it.

61 The image appears in your design and should have box around it so that you can resize it if needed, something like that:

Note: It's ok if the image looks out of focus. It will look fine once you accept it.

62 Accept the image by either clicking the tick icon in the Options bar or by pressing **Enter/Return** key on your keyboard.

63 Reposition the image of the camera to the left side of the design, below the green shape.

64 Rotate the image using **Edit > Transform > Rotate** so that it appears below the green shape, like that:

The camera on the poster has a glow around it. Let's create it now.

65 With the camera layer selected go to the bottom of the Layers panel, click the Fx icon, and choose **Outer Glow...**:

66 Keep adjusting the **Size** slider in the Elements section until you get the desired effect:

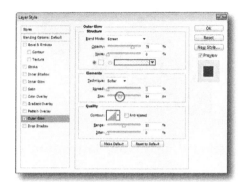

The original advert has a number of images of the same camera in different colours. That's what you're going to do now. To make things easier, and to show you how this is done, you are going to duplicate the layer with the image of the camera a number of times and colorise the cameras using Hue/Saturation adjustment.

67 With the layer with the camera selected duplicate it using **Layer > Duplicate Layer...**

68 Name the new layer **Camera Blue** and click OK.

69 In the Layers panel click and drag Camera Blue layer below the original camera layer:

70 Using Move tool reposition Camera Blue layer to the right and rotate it:

71 With Camera Blue layer selected apply **Hue/Saturation** adjustment layer and adjust **Hue** so that camera changes to blue colour:

Note: You may have noticed that as you were adjusting the Hue the colours of other objects also changed. That's because by default the adjustment layer affects all the layers below. You're going to deal with that now.

72 Still in the Properties panel, click clipping icon at the bottom of the panel to clip the adjustment layer to the image layer:

Now that the adjustment layer is being clipped to the layer below (the blue camera layer), it only affects the layer below (the blue camera layer).

This was easy, wasn't it? And it's such a great effect. I use Hue/Saturation a lot for colourising images. Now it's time to create another colour version of the camera.

73 Duplicate the original camera once again and name it **Camera Yellow**.

74 In the Layers panel click and drag Camera Yellow layer below the original camera layer.

75 Reposition and rotate the layer as in **Step 70**.

76 Add Hue/Saturation adjustment layer and change the colour of the camera to yellow as in **Step 71**.

77 Clip the adjustment layer to the image layer as in **Step 72**.

Now you should have three cameras in three different colours like this:

Note: Did you notice that as you were duplicating layers they were inheriting the Outer Glow effect? Now all of the camera layers have this effect.

78 Repeat the steps to add one more camera in another colour.

It's time to add some more text down below the cameras.

79 Select the layer with the gradient and then select the **Horizontal Type** tool.

80 Click in the lower left side of the advert and type the text as on the screenshot here:

81 Accept the text and then in the Options bar set the text alignment to left.

82 Highlight the first two lines with text **10x zoom** and make them much bigger than the rest of the text (click and drag with text tool over the first two lines to highlight them).

83 Place the cursor before the word zoom in the second line and press Spacebar a few times to indent the text as shown on the screenshot:

84 If you need to adjust the spacing between the lines of text use Character panel

(**Window > Character**):

85 The highlighted area is where you can change the spacing between the lines.

86 Give the entire text layer a slight **Drop Shadow**.

Next you're going to add another text layer with some of the highlights of the specifications of the camera.

87 With Horizontal Type tool selected, click below the text you have just added to create a new text layer.

88 Type the text as on the screenshot here:

89 Accept the text and reduce the size of needed so that the text is more or less the same size as the text **travel compact**.

90 Finally, in the lower right corner of the design, you're going to add one more text layer.

91 Click in the lower right corner of the design with Horizontal Type tool and type **Fujifilm Photography. Focused.**

This final text is going to be slightly blurred to create an interesting effect, especially with the word Focused in the text.

92 With the text layer selected choose **Filter > Blur > Gaussian Blur...**

Note: To apply a filter to the text, text will need to be rasterised and will not be editable any more as you are going to see now.

93 Photoshop will let you know that the text layer will need to be rasterised. Accept it by clicking **OK**:

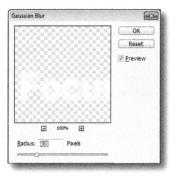

In **Photoshop CC**, you will see exactly the same dialogue box, with just one difference - the text on the top of the dialogue box will read Adobe Photoshop CC instead of Adobe Photoshop CS6 Extended.

94 When Gaussian Blur filter dialogue box opens add a few pixels blur and click OK:

The poster is almost finished. Just one more finishing touch. At the bottom of the poster you will add a green horizontal line.

95 Move the text layer you have created in the last few steps to the bottom right corner of the design.

96 Select **Line** tool:

97 In the Options bar set **Pick Tool mode** to Shape, **Fill** to green colour and **Stroke** to No Stroke:

98 Click on one edge of the document, hold the mouse button down and start dragging the cursor to the other edge of the document.

Note: Hold Shift key down as you are dragging to create a straight line. When you get to the other side of the document, release the mouse button first and then the Shift key.

99 Deselect the line layer to see what the line looks like.

100 If the line is not thick enough, choose Edit > Transform > Scale with the line layer selected.

101 Resize the line to make it thicker:

102 When done resizing accept the transformation (tick in the Options bar).

Your poster is done. Now you will finish this lesson with some tidying up in the design. You will group some layers next.

Layer Groups

Layer Groups in Photoshop are primarily used for grouping similar layers together. One of advantages of using layer groups is the ability to move all the layers in a layer group in one go instead of selecting all the layers and then moving them. Layer group can also be easily resized with all the layers inside the layer group being resized at the same time.

Note: Now in Adobe Photoshop CS6 you can also add Blend Modes to layer groups.

In this example you are working on it would be a good idea to group all the cameras together so if you decide to move them all or resize them, you can easily do it with a group.

103 Select all the layers with cameras and adjustment layers attached to them:

Note: You can just click on the top camera layer, hold Shift key down and click on the bottom camera layer. This will select all the layers in between.

104 With all the layers selected click the Layer Group icon at the bottom of the Layers panel (you can also press **Ctrl+G / Cmd+G**):

105 Now all the selected layers will be grouped:

106 Rename the group to **Cameras**.

Your design is finished. One final touch will be to tidy up a bit more in the Layers panel, mainly by positioning the layers as they appear in the design.

107 Rearrange the layers in the Layers panel (by dragging them around) so that the layers appearing at the top of the design appear at the top of the Layers panel.

You're done! Congratulations! One more lesson finished.

The last screenshot on the next page shows the design we have created.

Lesson 08

Panoramas

Things you are going to learn in this lesson are things like:

- Shooting Panoramas

- Creating a Panorama from a set of images

- Photomerge Layout Options

- Filling Missing Areas with Content-Aware Fill

- Cropping Panoramas

Shooting Panoramas

Let's start by explaining what panoramas are before we jump into creating them in Photoshop. Panoramas (or panoramic photographs as they're also called) are techniques of photography, using specialized equipment or software, that capture images with elongated fields of view.

Photomerge in Photoshop came a long way since it appeared and it is very good and very easy to use. Photomerge in Photoshop is used for stitching together images that create a panorama.

Before you start using Photomerge a few words about panoramas and taking photographs for panoramas.

Now, with digital cameras and mobile phones, there is no need for special cameras or lenses any more. You can create a great panorama from a series of images you take on your camera and then stitch them together using Photoshop.

The first step is to take a number of shots and you will need that for the exercise in this chapter. And, you can practise with your own images which is great. You can even take some photos from the window of your house or office.

Many cameras offer a feature of taking a panorama, but from what I've seen it leave much to be desired. What is even worse, they do not offer the opportunity to adjust the image manually at a later stage. It can be very frustrating if you believe you've taken the greatest panorama ever only to find out that there are visible connections between the photographs.

Once you've got your camera set up (best to use a DSLR camera or a digital compact, but you can use your mobile phone if you don't have a camera), you're ready to shoot some photos. When you start shooting, you need to make sure that all the images will overlap. Ideally, you would use a tripod as it allows you to level all the images. If you don't have one just try to hold the camera as steady as you can. Photoshop will align the images for you.

Here's an example of how the images should overlap (as a rule, the more they overlap the better):

Avoid taking photos at an angle, keep the camera straight. This will just make it harder to create a panorama and the final panorama will be smaller.

Keep the camera at the same position after taking each picture until you see the live preview on your camera's screen again. Then pick something near the edge of your scene like a building or a tree and move your camera to the side. Move your camera on a horizontal plane keeping the horizon in the same position as the previous picture. Make sure that the point you picked is still visible to create an overlap between the two pictures. Repeat this process until you've finished your panorama.

Note: Preview the pictures you've taken on your camera and check the horizon and if there is enough overlap between the pictures.

Your images for a panorama can be taken either on horizontal or vertical axis.

Some more tips for shooting panoramas:

- Use the same focal length for all pictures (if you use a zoom lens).

- Try not to move when taking pictures to get the same point of view.

- Try to keep the same exposure settings (not possible when you use a mobile phone).

Photomerge

Here are the images that I am going to use in this lesson:

1 Once you've taken the pictures for your panorama, download them onto your computer into a folder.

2 Open Photoshop if it's not currently open.

Before you create a panorama I will explain a few more things.

From a technical point of view, your images for a panorama should overlap around 25% or even more. Many Photoshop experts and photographers recommend around 40% overlap for panoramas. However, Photoshop will do a great job even if your images only overlap around 10%.

There are two ways of opening Photomerge command:

*   In Photoshop, File > Automate > Photomerge...

*   In Bridge, Tools > Photoshop > Photomerge...

As we are going to cover Bridge in detail in a later lesson, for now you will use Photoshop way.

3 Choose **File > Automate > Photomerge...**

This opens **Photomerge** dialogue box:

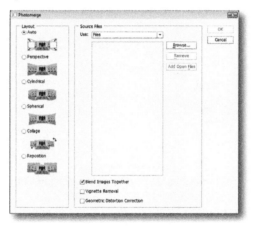

4 Click **Browse...** button to select the files for your panorama.

5 Select the files you want to use and accept them to go back to Photomerge dialogue box:

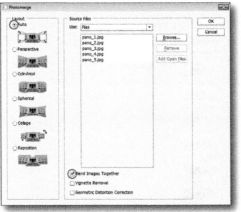

6 Leave Layout set to **Auto** and make sure that **Blend Images Together** option is

checked:

*Note: **Blend Images Together** option blends all the images together by adding layer masks to all the layers (images will appear on separate layers).*

Let me explain the **Photomerge Layout** options available in Photoshop CS6 and CC before we move on.

Photomerge Layout options:

Auto - Best for most situations, especially for shots of landscape panoramas. In this mode, Photoshop analyses the pictures and applies either a Perspective, Cylindrical, and Spherical layout, depending on which produces a better photomerge.

Perspective - It uses one of the images as the reference image. The other images are then transformed (repositioned, stretched or skewed as necessary) so that overlapping content across layers is matched.

Cylindrical - It makes sure that the images are aligned correctly to the horizontal axis. Good for very wide panoramas.

Spherical - It aligns and transforms the images as if they were inside of a sphere. Great for 260 degree panoramas.

Collage - It positions the images without transforming individual layers.

Reposition - It aligns the layers and matches overlapping content, but does not transform any of the source layers.

7 Click **OK**.

8 Photoshop starts opening the images and positioning them into the same document.

Note: If you use high resolution images, Photomerge may take long time to stitch the images together (especially if you use a slow computer with limited amount of RAM memory). Go and have some tea or coffee and let Photoshop do all the work.

Once Photoshop finishes you should see a beautiful panorama:

Have I mentioned that Photoshop does amazing job creating panoramas? Well, just look at the effect. It looks stunning. And you didn't have to do much, Photoshop did all the hard work.

Sometimes there will be gaps with missing pixels within a panorama and I have some here as well. It's actually really easy to take care of that and you're going to do it next.

9 Merge all the layers by choosing **Layer > Merge Layers**.

10 Using **Magic Wand** tool select the transparent areas on the edges of the panorama:

11 Expand your selection by **10** to **20** px using **Select > Modify > Expand**.

12 Choose **Edit > Fill**.

13 From Use drop-down menu choose **Content-Aware** and click **OK**:

After a moment you will see a beautiful panorama with no gaps on the edges of the document.

Note: If you use high resolution images and a lot of them, the panorama may take long to render. Here's an example of how big my panorama is and I only used five images:

It's almost 12,000 pixels long! And if printed, it would measure almost 5 meters in length! That's roughly a size of a wall at home, isn't it?

14 Choose **Select > Deselect**.

15 If you want to see how big your panorama is, choose **Image > Image Size...**

16 Save the image.

In **Photoshop CC**, Image Size dialogue box has changed and it looks a bit different now, but it's still in the same place under Image menu.

One of the big changes is that now, in Photoshop CC, you get a preview of the image inside the Image Size dialogue box (on the left side):

Because the panorama has really big dimensions keep in mind that when you save it the file may be really big, especially if you save it as a PSD or TIFF file.

I saved my panorama as a PNG file with no compression and the files size is almost 100MB:

panorama
PNG File
95.2 MB

Note: If you're preparing a panorama to be printed, save it as a JPEG file. It is the best choice for printing photographs, especially at high-street photo labs.

Here's another example of creating a panorama with Photomerge, but with different images. In this example, you will use images of a tight scene like a stadium or inside of a big house to see what else is possible with Photomerge.

Here are the images I'm going to use, the images of the Olympic Stadium in Barcelona:

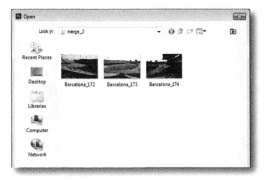

As you can see from the images, the perspective here is different. It is not a straight landscape image any more. And because of that, some options will need to be changed.

17 Copy the images you want to use to your computer (or you can access low resolution version of my images called barcelona).

18 In Photoshop, choose **File > Automate > Photomerge...**

19 Select the images for the panorama.

20 Keep Layout set to **Auto** and Click **OK** to accept the defaults.

21 Let Photoshop create a panorama and check the result.

Here's what I got. Not too bad for running it on Auto:

But you know what? We can do much better than that. And that's what you're going to do next.

22 You can keep the panorama open to compare if you have enough memory.

23 Choose **File > Automate > Photomerge...** again.

24 Choose the same images when Photomerge dialogue box opens.

25 This time change the Layout to **Cylindrical**:

26 Click **OK** to accept the other options.

Here's the final effect using Cylindrical Layout:

27 If you want to see both results (if you kept the first panorama), choose **Window > Arrange > 2-up Horizontal**.

28 Zoom out both images if needed so that you can see both.

So here's both of them on the same page (Auto on top, Cylindrical on bottom):

The second panorama looks much better and that's the one you will work on to finish the panorama.

29 Choose **Window > Arrange > Consolidate All to Tabs** to rearrange the documents' windows together.

30 Close the first panorama.

In the next few steps you will crop the panorama to remove transparent pixels.

31 Select **Crop** tool:

32 In the Options bar make sure that the Width and Height fields are blank:

33 Click and drag over the image to create a crop overlay over the image like this:

34 Accept the crop.

35 Save the file and you're done!

Congratulations! You have successfully finished another lesson and now you know how to quickly and easily create beautiful panoramas.

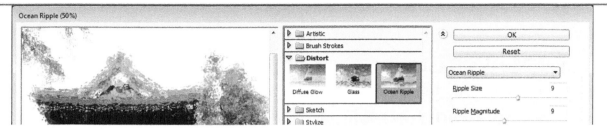

Lesson 09

Layer Masks

Things you are going to learn in this lesson are things like:

- Creating Layer Masks

- Creating Fading Effects with Layer Masks

- Working in Quick Mask Mode

- Using Refine Edge

- Filling with Patterns

- Clipping Images to Text

Layer Masks Basics

Masking layers is a very valuable technique used in compositing. Layer masks are often used for compositing multiple images into one image as well for local tonal or colour adjustments.

You can add a layer mask to a layer to hide a portion of an image (that's what you're going to do soon) and if you have any layers below, the layers will be revealed behind the hidden portion of an image.

You can create two types of layer masks:

- **Layer Masks** - resolution dependant, edited with selection tools or painting tools.

- **Vector Masks** - resolution independent, can be created with Pen tool.

Both kinds of layer masks are non-destructive. What does it mean? What it means is that you can re-edit them and you won't loose any pixels.

Layer masks can easily be edited so that you can add to an existing layer mask or subtract from it. Layer mask is grayscale (black and white and shades of gray) and the way it works with layer masks is:

- When you paint with **white** colour - you are making parts of an image visible,

- When you paint with **black** colour - you are making parts of an image hidden.

- When you paint with shades of **grey** - you are making parts of an image having variable levels of transparency.

White - revealing, Black - hiding.

When you add a layer mask, you can show or hide the entire layer (you just click the layer mask icon in the Layers panel) or you can add a layer mask to a selection, which will hide/show a part of an image.

Let's put the layer masks in practise. As the proverb says *"practise makes perfect"*.

Note: If you want to add a layer mask to a background layer, you will need to convert background layer to a regular layer first.

1 Start by creating a new document, set it to be **6 x 9 inch**, Resolution **300ppi** and name it **book_cover**:

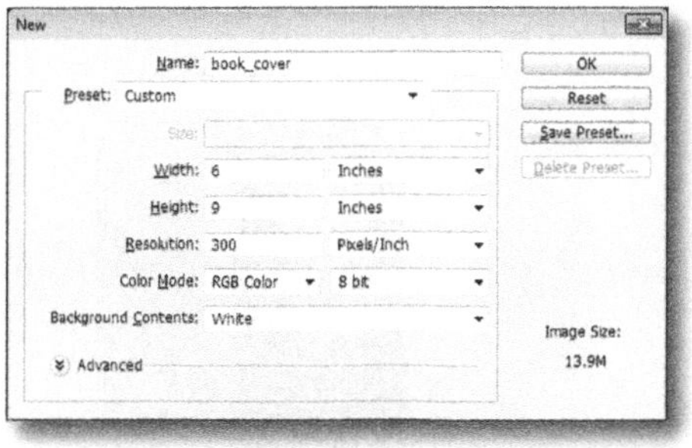

2 Download the image called **Door in ancient House** from stockxchange, it's free (or use your own image):

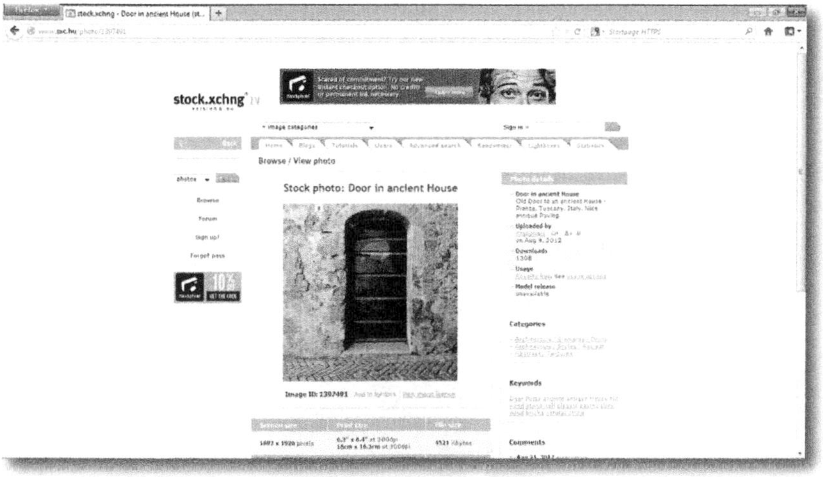

3 Place the image directly in your new document in Photoshop using **File > Place...**

4 Leave the image in the centre and using a selection tool of your choice select the door.

I used Quick Selection tool to get this:

The way it works with layer masks is that when you have a selection and you click on a layer mask icon, Photoshop will keep your current selection and hide everything else. So in this case, it's actually opposite of what we want to create because you will hide the door and place another image inside the door. So you will need to inverse the selection first.

5 Choose **Select > Inverse** to inverse the selection.

6 Click the layer mask icon at the bottom of the Layers panel to add a layer mask:

7 Image layer now has a layer mask next to it in the Layers panel and the door disappears:

The black and white rectangle next to the layer in the Layers panel is a layer mask.

8 Resize canvas to **6 x 8** inch using **Image > Canvas Size...** (keep Anchor in the centre):

9 When a message appears saying that the new canvas is smaller than the current canvas size, accept it by clicking **Proceed**:

Now that you've resized the canvas, it is time to add an image behind the image of the wall so that it will show through the door. By adding a layer mask to the image with the wall and the door you have restricted the view behind this image to just the area where the door was. That's an example of how we use layer masks in Photoshop.

For now, don't worry about the top and the bottom of the design. Keep the image centred. It's time to bring another image into the background and show it through the door.

10 Select the background layer in the Layers panel.

11 Place an image with a nice view using **File > Place...** For example, something like that:

12 Position the image behind the wall inside the door so that it shows through the door.

13 Accept the image by clicking tick icon in the Options bar or by pressing Enter/Return.

14 To make it into an interesting effect apply one of the filters from the Filter Gallery to the image within the door using **Filter > Filter Gallery...**

15 Accept the filter by clicking OK.

Notice that the filter becomes a Smart Filter. That's because when you place an image, it becomes a Smart Object automatically. And, because it's a Smart Filter, you can always re-edit it without loosing the settings and quality.

Fading Effects with Layer Masks

In the next few steps, you are going to add writing to the wall and fade it into the background with a layer mask and an interesting effect.

16 Select the top layer in the Layers panel.

17 Place an image **writing.jpg** into the design.

18 Accept the image.

19 Position the image with the writing on the left side of the design.

20 Scale the image down using **Edit > Transform > Scale** so that it fits on the left side next to the door:

21 Add a layer mask to the writing layer by just clicking on Add layer mask icon at the bottom of the Layers panel.

22 Click on the Layer Mask icon to make sure that it's selected:

23 Select **Gradient** tool:

24 Set your Foreground and Background colours to the defaults (black and white). You can just press **D** and then **X**:

25 In the Options bar set the gradient to **Foreground to Background** and **Radial Gradient**:

26 If your gradient is black to white (mine on the screenshot is white to black), check **Reverse** in the Options bar:

27 Click in the centre of the writing, hold the mouse button down and drag outwards to the edge of the writing image. Release the mouse button:

28 If you are not happy with the effect, re-apply the gradient.

29 Create a new layer and using Rectangular Marquee tool draw a rectangle covering the bottom of the page like that:

30 Fill the selection with a shade of grey using **Edit > Fill** and selecting **Color...** from Use drop-down menu.

31 Lower the opacity of the layer to make the grey rectangle semi-transparent.

32 Deselect the selection using **Select > Deselect**.

33 Type some text on top of the grey rectangle using **Horizontal Type** tool.

34 Add a layer effect to the text to give it more depth, for example **Bevel & Emboss**.

Now it's time for our main character for our book cover - a bear. You're going to "re-use" the image of the bear you used in previous lesson, the image called malta_2.jpg.

Quick Mask Mode

To me **Quick Mask Mode** is one of the least understood and used features in Photoshop. At the same time, it is a great and powerful feature that can be used for refining selections in Photoshop. Quick Mask Mode has been around for many years and I have been using it since I started working with Photoshop.

Often, I see Photoshop users click the Quick Mask Mode icon, notice that nothing special happens, and exit Quick Mask Mode and never use it again. And Quick Mask Mode is a powerful feature that is so useful for refining selections.

35 Select the top layer in the Layers panel.

36 Place image called **malta_2.jpg** using **File > Place**.

37 Accept the image so that it becomes a Smart Object straight away.

The first step is going to be to create a selection, an initial selection, and then you will use Quick Mask Mode to refine the selection.

38 Create a quick selection of the bear using a selection tool of your choice.

39 With the selection running click the **Quick Mask Mode** icon near the bottom of the Tools panel (it looks like the European Union flag):

*Note: You can also press **Q** on your keyboard to enter (and then exit) Quick Mask Mode.*

40 A part of the image goes red:

Quick Mask Mode colours explained:

- **Red colour overlay** (also referred to as rubylith colour) covers and protects the area outside the selection.

- **Transparent areas** keep the area of the selection unprotected.

So to explain the simple terms:

- **Transparent** is what you have **selected**,

- **Red overlay** is what you have **not selected**.

41 Zoom in closely to see the edges of your selection clearly.

42 Select **Brush** tool and set it to a small hard edged brush (**Hardness 100%**):

Slightly different drop-down menu for Brush tool in Photoshop CC:

43 Set the Foreground colour to **White** and paint over any area you missed in your selection (any area of the bear that appears to have the red overlay).

44 Set the Foreground colour to **Black** and paint over any area of the background that you selected.

*Note: You can quickly cycle through your foreground and background colours by pressing **X** on your keyboard. Once your foreground and background colours are set to black and white, use **X** to change your foreground colour to black and then white.*

45 When you're finished, the bear will need to have transparent overlay and the background red overlay like on a screenshot here:

That's before (on the left) and after (on the right):

46 When you're done, click Quick Mask Mode icon (or press Q) to exit Quick Mask Mode.

Now it's time to refine the edge of the selection. It's time for Refine Edge.

Refine Edge

47 Select one of the selection tools and in the Options bar you will notice **Refine Edge** button:

Note: Another way to access Refine Edge dialogue box is to use the menu: Select > Refine Edge...

48 Click Refine Edge button to open **Refine Edge** dialogue box:

We'll take the options one by one. This will make it easier to understand Refine Edge as everything is organised in the order in which you're supposed to work with it.

View Mode

This option allows you to change how the selection is displayed. As you move the cursor over the options a tooltip appears describing what each option does:

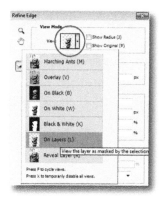

49 Choose **On Layers** from the View Mode drop-down menu.

When you choose On Layers from the View Mode drop-down menu, you will see what the object will look like once you refine the edge. If there are layers behind the object, you will see them behind it.

Show Radius displays the selection border where edge refinement occurs.

Show Original displays the original selection for comparison.

50 Leave both above options unchecked.

Adjust Edge

Smooth - Reduces irregular areas in your selection border to create a smooth outline.

Feather - Blurs the transition between the selection and the pixels around the selection.

Contrast - Increases the contrast on the edges of your selection.

Shift Edge - Moves selection borders inward with negative values or outward with positive ones.

51 Readjust the settings to improve your selection.

In my case, I changed the following settings:

Smooth - 39

Contrast - 14%

52 Check the quality of your selection in detail:

53 In the bottom section of Refine Edge, under Output choose **New Layer with Layer Mask** from the Output To drop-down menu.

54 Reposition and scale down the bear using **Edit > Transform > Scale**.

Now, let's back up for a moment. Notice what happened in your Layers panel. Did you notice that you now have two layers with the bear?

One of the layers is hidden (the original) and there is another layer with a layer mask next to it. Now that you know how to work with Quick Mask Mode, it is pretty much the same with layer masks.

55 If your layer mask needs refinement, click on the layer mask to select it, choose a Brush tool and paint with black brush on the background to hide it or with white brush on the bear.

56 Keep the other bear layer hidden as you may need it.

57 In the Layers panel drag the bear layer below the layer with grey overlay at the bottom of the page so that the bear appears behind it:

The top of the design doesn't have any content. In the next few steps, you're going to fill the top of the page with a pattern and then add a book title on the top.

58 Create a New Layer on the top of the Layers panel.

59 With the layer selected draw a rectangle marquee covering the top of the page using Rectangular Marquee tool like that:

60 Fill the layer with a pattern using **Edit > Fill...**, and in the Fill dialogue box choose **Pattern** from the Use drop-down menu:

61 Choose one of the patters that appear under Custom Pattern and click OK.

62 Remove the selection by choosing **Select > Deselect**.

63 Rename the layer.

64 Select Horizontal Type tool and type the name for your book.

For now, don't worry about the colour of the text. Just make sure that it's a colour you can see.

65 Format the text with a font family of your choice.

Note: For the effect that you are going to add in just a moment to work make sure that your text is big and bold as you are going to place an image inside the text. By setting the text to be big and bold you will be able to see the image inside the text.

In the next few steps you are going to centre the text on the page with some help from Photoshop.

Here's how you can centre the text in Photoshop.

66 In the Layers panel select the text layer you have just created.

67 Holding down Ctrl on Windows (Cmd on Mac) select the Background layer.

Now both layers will be selected.

68 Select **Move** tool and the alignment icons will appear in the Options Bar:

69 Click the **Align horizontal centers** icon to align text to the centre.

Clipping Images

Clipping images to text is a very interesting effect that I first saw and learnt how to do years ago when I was working for a photo lab in London. It used to be a very popular effect for families where parents had the name of their baby printed with images inside the letters.

And that's the kind of effect you are going to recreate here with image filling the letters of the name of the book.

70 Select the layer with the text.

71 Place an image of your choice using **File > Place...**

Note: It's important that you place an image (you could also copy and paste it) directly above the text layer. That's why you have selected the text layer first.

72 Accept the image and position it on top of the text. The image needs to cover the text:

Make sure that you position the image so that the text is hidden behind it. The image can be as big as you want but at least the same width as the text.

73 In the Layers panel right-click the image layer (Smart Object layer if you used Place...) and choose Create Clipping Mask.

And voila! The image will now only appear behind the text because the image is now clipped to the text layer.

Because both the image and the text appear on separate layers, you can still easily reposition or rotate them at any time.

Final touch to the text and the clipped image - adding a Layer Style.

74 Add a Layer Style to the text, Drop Shadow or Bevel & Emboss.

The last part of this chapter will involve placing the design on the top of the image with the book (on the cover of the book) so that it looks like a real book cover.

75 Open **books.jpg**.

76 Back to your book cover design save the file.

77 Merge visible layers in the book cover design using **Layer > Merge Visible** (or use Ctrl+Shift+E / Cmd+Shift+E).

78 Choose Select > All and copy the cover design (**Edit > Copy** or **Ctrl+C / Cmd+C**).

79 Navigate to books.jpg image.

80 Paste the cover design using **Edit > Paste** or **Ctrl+V / Cmd+V**.

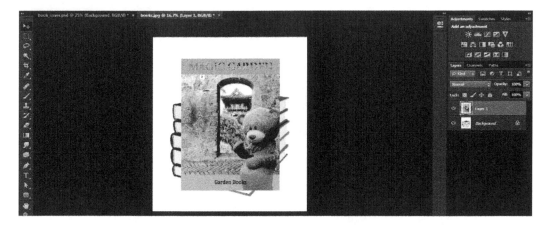

81 Scale the image down a bit and accept it.

82 With the cover image layer selected choose **Edit > Free Transform**.

83 Hold **Ctrl** key on Windows (**Cmd** key on Mac) down and start dragging the corners of the cover image to match with the corners of the book cover behind like this:

84 When you're done with all the corners the image should look like this:

85 Accept the transformation.

86 To finish the design add Bevel & Emboss to the cover layer.

87 In the **Layer Style** dialogue box set the following options:

>   **Style: Emboss**
>   **Technique: Smooth**
>   **Size: ca. 29 px**
>   **Soften: 0**

This is your final design.

You're done! Congratulations! One more lesson finished.

Lesson 10

Correcting Images

Things you are going to learn in this lesson are things like:

•   Cropping Scanned Images

•   Straightening Images

•   Removing Red Eyes

•   Correcting Highlights and Shadows

•   Correcting Lens Distortions

•   Sharpening

Cropping Scanned Images

So you've scanned an image, maybe an old photo of you or your family. What if the image was not placed properly on the scanning plate? What if the entire scanning plate was scanned with a lot of empty space around the image? Or maybe you've scanned three or four images in one go.

That's where cropping comes in.

Here's a scan that I am going to work on:

Clearly this image needs some work. It will need to be rotated first and then cropped.

1 Open an image of your choice.

2 In this case, with my image, I will need to rotate it first so I'm going to choose **Image > Image Rotation > 180°**.

I'm going to focus on the image on the right, that's why I've rotated the image by 180 degrees.

3 With your image rotated select **Crop** tool:

4 In the Options bar make sure that there are no values for Width and Height:

Note: This option is very useful if you want to crop an image to certain image dimensions, e.g. 4 x 6 inch.

Here's the Options bar for Crop tool in **Photoshop CC**:

Again a slight rearrangement of options in Photoshop CC. Following the last step, if you're using Photoshop CC, make sure there are no values in the fields for width and height.

5 Let's say we want to print this image in standard size 4 x 6 inch. Type **4in** and **6in** in these fields for Width and Height.

In **Photoshop CC**, click the drop-down menu where it reads **Ratio** and choose **W x H x Resolution**:

Then, type the values **4in** and **6in** the fields next to the drop-down menu.

6 You will now see a crop overlay that will display the crop preview for the specified size:

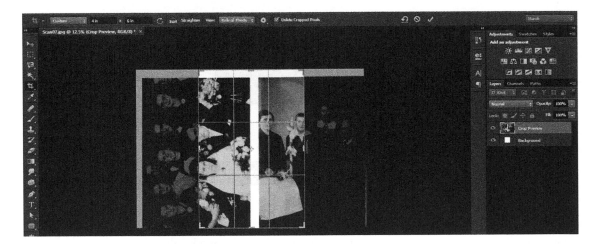

7 Click inside the crop overlay and drag to reposition it so that it matches the image.

8 You may need to resize the crop overlay if it doesn't fit the image entirely.

Crop tool is a very useful tool when working with images. And there are so many different things you can do with it.

Like in this example, as I moved the crop overlay (set to 4 x 6 inch), I've noticed that the image has a slightly different aspect ratio from the crop overlay, as shown here:

In this case, you can clearly see that if the image is printed as 4 x 6 inch print, some parts of the image will be cropped when printed. So what do I mean when I say that Crop tool is such a useful feature in this case?

Think about it. If you can crop an image to a certain dimension in Photoshop and the crop overlay doesn't cover the entire image (like in this case), you will know that something will need to be cropped when printed. If you crop the image in Photoshop, you can decide what to crop, in other words what to loose from the image when printed. If you have the printer crop and print the image, you have no control over what gets cropped from the printed image, it may as well be the top or the bottom of the image (or even both).

9 In this case I need to crop one of the sides so there is no white on the top.

In this case I'm cropping image on the right as there is space on the right edge of the image:

10 Once you've set the crop overlay accept the crop by either clicking the tick icon in the Options bar or press **Enter / Return** on your keyboard.

If you have used Photoshop in the past you may have noticed that something is missing in the Options bar for the Crop tool. Yes, it's the resolution. So what do you do? How do you crop the image to a certain resolution as well as certain dimensions? Well, there is a solution.

Note: This technique is for **Photoshop CS6 only** *as Photoshop CC brings back the Resolution field.*

11 If you want to crop the image to certain resolution, as you set the crop options (dimensions), click on the drop-down menu next to the dimensions fields:

12 From the drop-down menu choose **Size & Resolution....**

13 In the **Crop Image Size & Resolution** dialogue box you can type in resolution:

14 You can even save the crop settings as a preset by checking **Save as Crop Preset** option.

Now in Photoshop CS6 there is another new very interesting feature - **Delete Cropped Pixels**:

Selecting this option permanently deletes all the pixels when you crop the image. This may sound like a proper way of working but bear in mind that when you use this option, the pixels are being deleted permanently. In other words, you are working destructively.

There is a way to work non-destructively by leaving Delete Cropped Pixels option unchecked. In this situation, Photoshop will simply hide the pixels when you crop the image and you will be able to go back and change your crop at any time.

There is one more option that I want to explain before you move on - **Crop Overlay**.

As you start cropping the image you notice a crop overlay appear, kind of like a grid. By default, Photoshop CS6 uses **Rule of Thirds** for the overlay. What is Rule of Thirds you may be asking?

Rule of Thirds divides an image into nine imaginary, evenly sized rectangles. When compositing an image, the main subject of the image should be placed where these lines intersect.

Rule of Thirds is not the only crop overlay available in Photoshop CS6. It is one of many overlays available.

15 Click on **View** crop-down menu in the Options bar:

In **Photoshop CC** you click on this icon:

One of the options on the drop-down menu is **Grid**, which displays more detailed grid appear over the image as a crop preview.

*Note: You can also cycle through different overlays by pressing **O** on your keyboard.*

At the bottom of the list of crop overlays there is one more section where you can choose when you want the overlays to appear and if you want the overlay to appear.

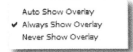

Auto Show Overlay option will only appear when you are resizing the crop box or when you are repositioning the image.

As we are still talking about the Crop tool, let's have a look at one more option - **Straightening images**.

Straightening Images

How about straightening images with Crop tool? I know what you're thinking. Isn't there a straighten tool or something in Photoshop? Well, there is in Crop tool options.

Photoshop gives you a number of options for straightening images. To start with, you can drag an outline with Crop tool, position the cursor outside one of the corner handles and drag to rotate the image (and straighten at the same time) manually.

Or you could use the **Straighten** option in the Options bar.

16 Open an image that needs some straightening.

17 Select Crop tool and in the Options bar click **Straighten**:

18 Find something in your image that should straight either horizontally or vertically.

19 Click, hold the mouse button down, and drag to define the straight line in the image:

20 Release the mouse button and Photoshop will straighten the image for you.

21 Accept the crop.

Here's my after:

22 If you have made any mistake when cropping the image, you can undo what you have done using **Edit > Undo**.

Note: You can also reset what you have done with Crop tool using Reset button in the Options bar:

Reset button will reset the crop box as well as aspect ratio and rotation.

23 Accept the crop and close the image.

Red Eye Removal

There are so many ways of removing red eyes in Photoshop that if you were to ask a number of Photoshop users how to remove red eyes from images, you would most probably get a number of different answers.

How do people get red eyes on images? Red eyes appear on images when a camera's flash reflects off the back of the person's eye. It usually appears when a person looks straight into the camera.

Many cameras have a feature called "red eye reduction", which uses a pre-flash to make person's irises a bit smaller before the main flash occurs. Not the most practical feature and in many situations it just doesn't work as the person taking picture would want.

In this lesson, you are going to use two techniques for red eye removal:

- Red Eye tool

- Color Replacement tool.

Why two techniques? Both techniques work well but what you may find is that in some situations one technique may work better than the other.

Red Eye tool

24 Open an image that needs some red eye removal.

25 Zoom into the image to see the eyes clearly.

26 Select **Red Eye tool**:

27 There aren't many options in the Options bar so you can leave them on their defaults:

28 With Red Eye tool selected just click on the red eye.

29 Repeat the last step for the other red eyes in the image.

That's my Before:

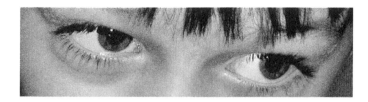

and After:

As you can see, in just a moment, in most cases with a single click, you can remove red eyes from images you are working on.

Note: You can click and drag over the red eye with Red Eye tool as well.

Color Replacement tool

Color Replacement tool allows you to change the colour as well as hue and saturation and you apply it by manually brushing over the eyes. Unlike Red Eye tool, which is pretty much automatic, with Color Replacement tool you get more control. Another great feature of Color Replacement tool is that it will try to preserve the original texture while it's changing the colours.

30 If you're still working on the same image, undo what you have done. Assuming you haven't saved your image, you can use **File > Revert**.

31 Select **Color Replacement** tool:

32 Duplicate the Background layer.

Note: You are duplicating the Background layer so that you don't work on the original layer and if anything goes wrong you can easily delete the duplicate layer.

33 In the Options bar from the Brush Preset drop-down menu choose a hard edged brush (high **Hardness**) and low **Spacing**:

34 Set your Foreground colour to the colour you want to use for colour replacement.

35 Back to the Options bar, click on the Painting Mode drop-down menu to select what colour characteristics the tool applies to. Choose **Color**.

Color Painting Mode seems to create the best results, but as usual feel free to experiment.

36 In the next set of icons click **Sampling: Continuous** button:

Sampling: Continuous

Sampling options for Color Replacement tool

Sampling: Continuous will only apply the Foreground colour to the pixels that the brush moves over, which will allow you to replace both lighter and darker pixels within the eyes.

Sampling: Once will sample the pixel when you click first and will apply the Foreground colour to pixels that match the sampled colour (excluding different shades of the same colour).

Sampling: Background Swatch will only replace colours that similar to your current Background colour.

37 From the Limits drop-down menu choose **Contiguous**.

Limits options

Contiguous - it colorises pixels under the cursor including neighbouring pixels.

Discontiguous - it colorises only the pixels under the cursor.

Find Edges - it colorises pixels under the cursor and keeps the colour replacement within the shape.

38 Keep the **Tolerance** quite low, around 30 to 50.

Tolerance sets the range of colours to be colorised. Low tolerance will only colorise pixels that are close to the sampled colour. High tolerance will colorise a wide range of colours.

39 Keep **Anti-alias** checked.

Anti-alias option creates smoother transitions between the original colours and the replacement colours.

40 If you use a pressure sensitive pen and tablet, like Wacom tablet I use, click **Tablet Pressure Controls Size** at the end of the Options bar:

Always use Pressure for Size. When off, Brush Preset controls pressure

41 Make sure you have the layer selected and start painting over the areas that need to be recolorised.

Note: Remember that you can change the size of the brush by pressing square bracket keys ([and]). Left bracket key ([) makes the brush smaller and right bracket key (]) makes it bigger.

Highlights and Shadows

Shadows/Highlights adjustment has been around for a number of years (Adobe introduced it back in Photoshop CS). Since it was introduced, it became popular with photographers because of its ability to bring back the details in shadow and highlight areas.

One of the challenges Photoshop users had with Shadows/Highlights was that by default it would only show two controls:

And what many users were doing was they were cancelling the dialogue box when the image wasn't looking good and there were only two sliders within the Shadows/Highlights. To many users, default view of the Shadows/Highlights dialogue box looked a bit like Brightness/Contrast with its two controls. The real power of Shadows/Highlights, however, is revealed when you dive into the advanced options and that's what you're going to do in here.

Most adjustments in Photoshop CS6 are now available as adjustment layers that can be accessed through the Adjustments panel. However, Shadows/Highlights is not available in the Adjustment panel.

Shadows/highlights is one these few adjustments that are not available as adjustment layers. Since it's only available through the Image > Adjustments menu, remember that it will permanently alter the image, destructively. To protect the original image from permanent changes, you will work on a duplicate layer.

42 Open an image that you want to work on.

43 Duplicate the Background layer using **Ctrl/Cmd+J** or **Layer > Duplicate Layer...**

44 Rename the duplicate layer and keep it selected.

45 Choose **Image > Adjustments > Shadows/Highlights...**

This brings up the Shadows/Highlights dialogue box. If you haven't worked with Shadows/Highlights on your computer yet and if you haven't made any changes to the dialogue box, you should see a simple dialogue box with just two sliders like this:

The default value for Shadows is 50% which is usually too high creating washed out shadows and that's often the reason why people think that the adjustment doesn't work and cancel the dialogue box. Don't let the default options put you off as Shadows/Highlights can be a very good and very useful adjustment if put to proper use.

46 Start by setting Shadows slider to **0%** (Highlights should be at **0%** by default so leave it as it is).

47 When both sliders are set to 0% you should see no difference in the image from the original. Try ticking and unticking Preview checkbox to see that the image doesn't change.

48 Click Show More Options in the bottom left corner of the dialogue box:

This option will expand the dialogue box and show a lot of other options available. I know that at the first sight the expanded version of the dialogue box may appear to be too much with so many options available when in the simpler version there were only two sliders.

49 Have a closer look at the options available.

If you look closely at the options available, you will notice that the dialogue box is divided into two sections with the same options: **Amount**, **Tonal Width** and **Radius**.

Using the first section, **Shadows**, you can bring back the shadows details in the image.

Using the second section, **Highlights**, you can bring back the highlights details in the image.

Using the last section, **Adjustments**, you can adjust the image.

Shadows section explained:

Amount - it controls how much brightening you want to apply to the shadows. The more you move the slider to the right the more shadows you will recover.

50 Start dragging the **Amount** slider in the Shadows section and notice how the shadows are being recovered.

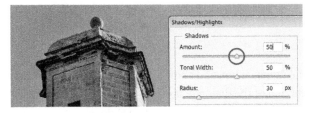

Simply by dragging the Amount slider I have managed to bring back a lot of details in the shadows on the side of the tower.The image looks so much better.

Tonal Width - it controls the range of tonal values that are affected. When you keep the value down only the darkest areas of the image are adjusted.

51 Look at the image as you drag the **Tonal Width** slider to the right to determine which value looks best with the image you are using.

Radius - it controls how the area you are adjusting will blend with the rest of the photo. When you keep the value down the photo may appear looking flat and you may see harsh transitions between adjusted area and unadjusted area.

52 Drag the **Radius** slider to adjust the blending and keep an eye on the image.

53 Once you've adjusted the Radius, you may want to go back and readjust other settings.

These are my settings for the photo I'm working on:

At this point, most Photoshop users click OK to accept the changes as the image starts looking really good. Yes, most Photoshop users use Shadows/Highlights just for correcting shadows and they leave highlights alone.

Highlights section

Highlights section, found below the Shadows section, was designed to reveal any missing details within the highlights areas within the photo. It contains exactly the same sliders: **Amount**, **Tonal Width** and **Radius**. And you know how to use these sliders already since you used them on the shadows.

In this case, Amount will determine the amount of darkening applied to the highlights. Be careful when working with highlights as they usually tend to reduce the contrast within the photo.

54 Adjust the sliders in the **Highlights** section using the same steps you used for Shadows.

Once you've finished adjusting highlights and shadows, if you find that your image lost some of the colour saturation, you can use **Color Correction** slider at the bottom of the dialogue box.

55 If you want to increase the colour saturation of the photo drag the **Color Correction** slider to the right.

I have slightly increased the color correction to 40.

56 Finally, to increase contrast in midtone areas, use **Midtone Contrast** slider:

57 And that's it. Click **OK** to accept the changes.

58 Because you were working on a separate layer, you can hide and show the duplicate to preview before and after.

59 Close the image.

Lens Distortions

There will be times when you will need to deal with lens distortions in your images with distortions like **barrel distortions** or **vignetting** or **chromatic abberations**. What are these distortions? Let me explain.

Barrel distortions - it is a defect of a lens that causes the straight lines in the image to bow out towards the edges of an image.

If the lines bend inwards, towards the centre of an image, this is called **pincushion distortion**.

Here's what **barrel distortions** and **pincushion distortions** look like:

barrel distortion   pincushion distortion

Vignetting - it is a defect of a lens that causes the corners of the image to darken (some photographers seem to love this effect).

Chromatic abberations - these appear as a colour fringe along the edges of the objects. It is caused by the lens focusing on different colours in different planes.

Lens Correction filter fixes many of the common faults/distortions like the ones mentioned above. To work efficiently, Lens Correction filter needs to access EXIF data from the camera to detect what camera and lens were used for capturing a photo so that it can find a matching lens profile to deal with the distortions.

Note: Lens Correction filter only works in 8-bit and 16-bit RGB and Grayscale mode.

First, you are going to try to correct the image distortions automatically. If this doesn't help, you can adjust the options manually. If Lens Corrections filter doesn't manage to detect EXIF data from the image you will need to use manual adjustments.

How do you find EXIF data in the image? Here's how.

60 Open the image that you want to work with or open church.jpg from the images folder.

61 To check EXIF data choose **File > File Info...**

62 Click **Camera Info** category to access EXIF data:

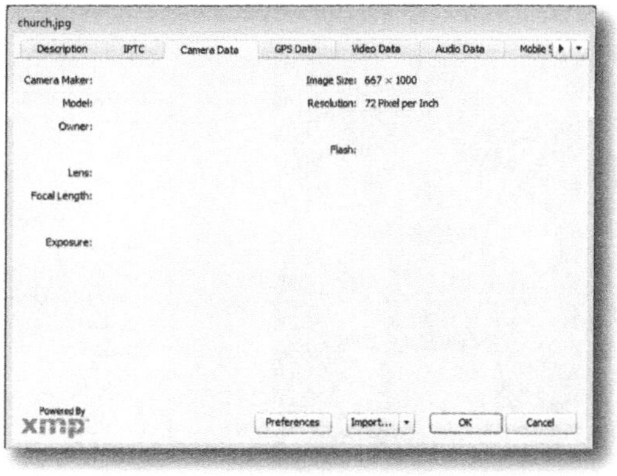

In this case, the camera didn't seem to register EXIF data as there is no camera model or lens model. So it looks like you will need to adjust the distortions in the image manually.

63 Click **OK** to close the File Info dialogue box.

64 Duplicate the background layer and select the duplicate.

65 Choose **Filter > Lens Correction...**

Lens Correction filter window opens:

Here's a nice trick in Lens Correction filter:

66 Click on the magnification drop-down menu and choose **Fit on Screen**:

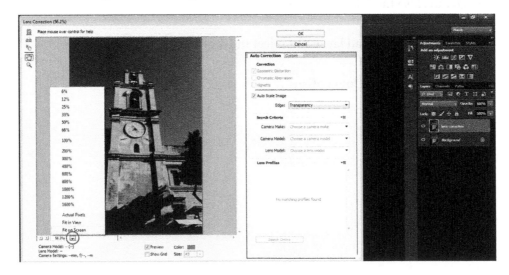

Now the Lens Correction window will fill the entire screen.

67 By default Lens Correction window opens with **Auto Correction** tab active:

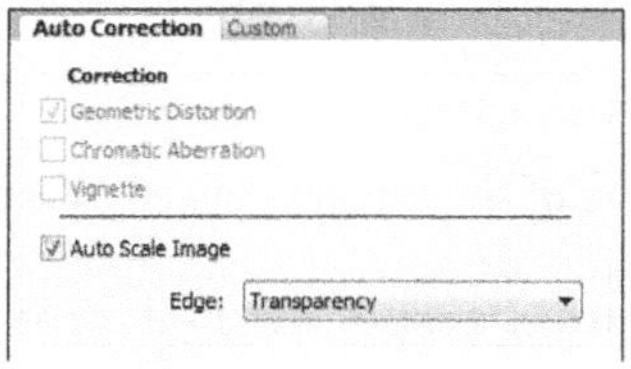

68 Because Photoshop didn't detect any EXIF data, there will be no options displayed in the bottom section of **Auto Correction** area of Lens Correction.

69 Click **Custom** tab on the right side of the window.

This will display all available options for lens correction as shown here:

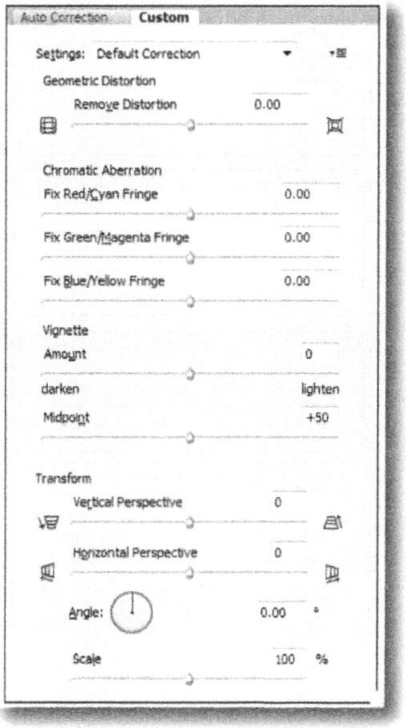

Lens Correction - Custom options:

Remove Distortion - it corrects barrel distortions or pincushion distortions. You can move the slider to straighten vertical and horizontal lines.

Chromatic Aberration - it corrects colour fringing by adjusting the sizes of colour channels in relation to one another.

Vignette - it corrects darkened corners of the images caused by lenses' faults.

Transform (Vertical and Horizontal Perspective) - it corrects the image perspective by making vertical or horizontal lines parallel.

Scale - it adjusts the image scale either up or down. The image's pixel dimensions don't change.

70 This image looks as if it is falling down away from you so use **Vertical Perspective** slider to straighten it:

You need to be careful when adjusting the image as it may loose some of its quality. It may become slightly out of focus.

71 Once you've adjusted the Vertical Perspective, adjust **Horizontal Perspective** as well.

72 Click OK when done.

Here's my before (on the left) and after (on the right):

Next, I will show you how it works when Photoshop manages to detect the EXIF data from the image and corrects the perspective automatically!

73 Open **myBooks.jpg** from the Images folder.

74 Duplicate the Background layer.

75 With the duplicate layer selected choose **Filter > Lens Correction...**

76 When Lens Correction opens, it applies the adjustments automatically reading the metadata information about the lens and camera used:

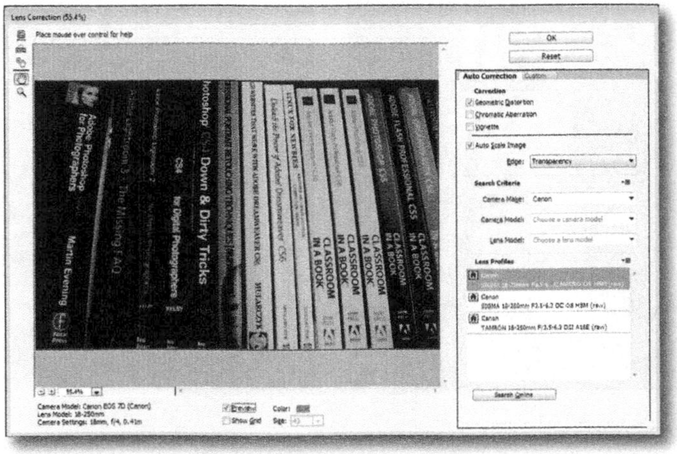

Lens Correction found the relevant lens profile for the camera and lens I used: Sigma 18-250mm OS HSM lens on a Canon EOS 7D camera. And it corrected distortions automatically! How great is that?

Photoshop CS6 supports most lenses and cameras found on the market. Just check for yourself by clicking on Camera Model and Lens Model drop-down menus:

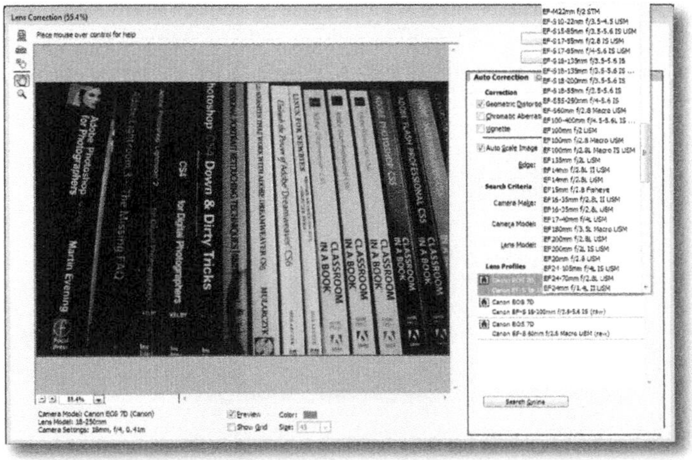

Note: The list of supported lenses is much longer than what you see here. And these are just Canon lenses. Add to it Nikon and Sigma and others and the list will be massive. Very impressive what Adobe accomplished here.

77 Check and uncheck **Preview** box at the bottom of the dialogue box to see before and after to notice how distortions were fixed by Lens Correction.

78 When done click **OK** and close the image.

Sharpening

When working with digital images, at one point you will need to sharpen them. You will need to sharpen all of your images sooner or later. Even if you use high quality and high resolution camera, your images will need some work. The same when it comes to scans, the images will be slightly off focus when being scanned. In case of digital cameras, the images will be slightly out of focus because of the anti-aliasing filters that are used on the cameras sensors.

How much should you sharpen? The short answer is: It depends. If you capture your images as JPEGs, your camera will sharpen the image for you as well as it will apply some noise reduction.

If you capture your images in raw, the images will have no processing applied to them since raw images are unprocessed. Any sharpening would need to be done in Photoshop or in Camera Raw (more on Camera Raw in the next chapter).

If you work with images that were scanned, the scanner may have applied some sharpening to the images. Some scanners do this by default so you would need to change the settings on your scanner to disable any sharpening.

Camera Raw sharpening

Since we're going to cover Camera Raw in detail in the next chapter, I am not going to cover sharpening using Camera Raw. For now, just so you know, there have been many improvements in Camera Raw 7 that offer better sharpening and image processing. And as you know, Camera Raw processes not just raw files but also JPEGs. Camera Raw also brings new and improved image processing called **Process 2012**, which we will cover in the next chapter as well.

Now, let's do some sharpening in Photoshop and then, we'll cover sharpening in Camera Raw in the next chapter.

Smart Sharpen

Some people when they think about sharpening images in Photoshop, they think about Unsharp Mask. We have been using Unsharp Mask filter for many years, but how about Smart Sharpen? Smart Sharpen filter seems to be a bit slower than Unsharp Mask, but if used correctly it can produce very good results. Let's open an image and I will explain the options.

79 Open an image that needs sharpening.

I'm going to use this image:

80 Duplicate the background layer and select it.

81 Convert the duplicate layer to a Smart Object (right-click on layer and choose **Convert to Smart Object**) so that you could edit the filter later on.

82 Choose **Filter > Sharpen > Smart Sharpen...**

Here's Smart Sharpen in all its glory:

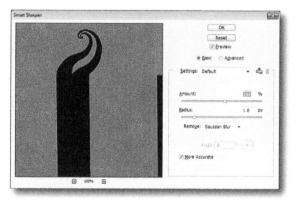

Remove drop-down menu near the bottom of the dialogue box offers three options:

• **Gaussian Blur,**

• **Lens Blur,**

• **Motion Blur**.

83 Set it to **Gaussian Blur** so that the filter will work like Unsharp Mask filter.

Note: Gaussian Blur is the default setting. Motion Blur may help with motion blur in images and Lens Blur may help with lens blur.

84 Make sure that **More Accurate** is checked for better quality sharpening.

85 Now you can use **Amount** and **Radius** sliders to adjust sharpening.

Let me explain these options first.

Amount and Radius

Both sliders control sharpening that is being applied and how the sharpening is being distributed within the image.

Amount slider - increases or decreases sharpening.

Radius slider - determines the width of the halos that are created around the edges. Small value will have little effect on the soft edges within the photo. Use values around 1.0,

86 Adjust the **Amount** slider initially to **100%**.

87 Set **Radius** initially to **1.0**.

If you increase the Radius, here's what's going to happen with the halos around the edges:

88 Adjust the **Radius** slider to sharpen the image without creating too many halos around the edges.

89 Click OK to accept the changes.

If you need to change the settings you can double-click on the name of the filter in the Layers panel at any time.

Smart Sharpen in **Photoshop CC**:

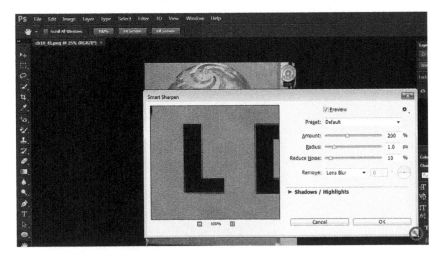

One of the first things you will notice when you open Smart Sharpen in Photoshop CC is the big preview window on the left side of the dialogue box. But it doesn't stop there with Photoshop CC. Turn the page over to find out about a great new feature within Smart Sharpen Dialogue box in Photoshop CC.

One of great new features in Smart Sharpen in Photoshop CC is the ability to resize the window! You just place the cursor in the bottom right corner of the dialogue box and when it changes to double arrow, click and drag to resize it, as shown below:

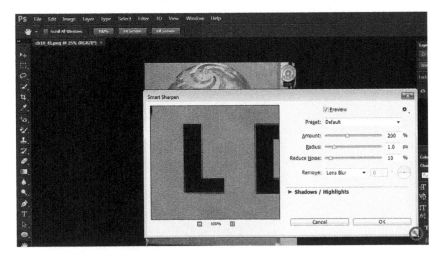

Let's move on to another great feature.

As you noticed, there are a number of new options within the dialogue box. But Photoshop CC gives you an option to work with Smart Sharpen the way you used to work in Photoshop CS6. How?

By clicking on the gear icon in the top right corner and ticking **Use Legacy** box:

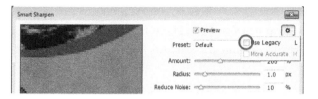

90 Let's try something. Tick **Use Legacy** box.

91 Increase **Amount** to 300 or more.

92 Tick and untick **Use Legacy** and notice how the quality of the image changes.

Now in Photoshop CC, the noise within the image has been drastically reduced, when compared to Smart Sharpen in Photoshop CS6. You can even push the Amount slider higher and higher without getting much of halos as we used to in Photoshop CS6.

Here's Smart Sharpen in Photoshop CS6 and Photoshop CC compared:

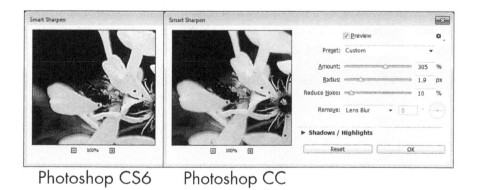

Photoshop CS6   Photoshop CC

And now you even have **Reduce Noise** slider which you can use to reduce noise in the image.

Shadows / Highlights in Smart Sharpen

And, just to add one more great new feature in Photoshop CC, now in Smart Sharpen you can also adjust sharpening of dark and light areas using the Shadows / Highlights section at the bottom of the Smart Sharpen dialogue box:

Here are the options available in **Shadows / Highlights** section:

- **Fade Amount** - the amount of sharpening being applied in the shadows or highlights.

- **Tonal Width** - the range of tones in the shadows or highlights that are modified. Lower values will only modify the darker areas in the shadows and the lighter areas in the highlights.

- **Radius** - the size of the area around each pixel that is being used to determine shadows or highlights.

93 Readjust the sliders in **Shadows / Highlights** section if required.

94 Close the image when done.

This last part of the lesson showed you how you can sharpen the images in Photoshop using Smart Sharpen, however the best way to sharpen images is to use Camera Raw giving you the best results. And you can edit JPEGs in Camera Raw as well so there is no reason why you shouldn't do sharpening in Camera Raw. And that's what we're going to cover in the chapter on Camera Raw.

You're done! Congratulations! One more lesson finished.

Lesson 11

Adobe Bridge

Things you are going to learn in this lesson are things like:

- Exploring Bridge Interface

- Slideshow Mode

- Bridge Filters

- Exploring Metadata

- Downloading Images with Photo Downloader

- Star Rating and Labelling

- Collections

- Output to PDF

- File Export with Image Processor

Adobe Bridge Interface

As you progress working in Photoshop and getting more experience, you will gather more and more images on your hard drive. You will need something more than just Explorer or Finder for managing and finding images to work with. You will need an application that will allow you to organise your images and even preview them quickly without opening additional applications. Maybe even an application that will allow you to import photos from your camera or memory card. Fortunately, Bridge fits into all this with all the above mentioned features.

The good news is if you have Photoshop you have Bridge as well. Bridge ships with Photoshop as well as with many other Adobe applications including all Creative Suite editions. You can use Bridge to open images with Camera Raw as well because Camera Raw works either in Photoshop or in Bridge. Because these last two chapters focus on Bridge and Camera Raw, you're going to spend time in these last two chapters in Bridge. And, Bridge can preview images as well as videos.

So let's have a look at Bridge. You're going to start by setting Bridge Preferences first.

1 Start Bridge from your Programs or Applications.

Note: You can also start Bridge from Photoshop (if it's running) using File > Browse in Bridge.

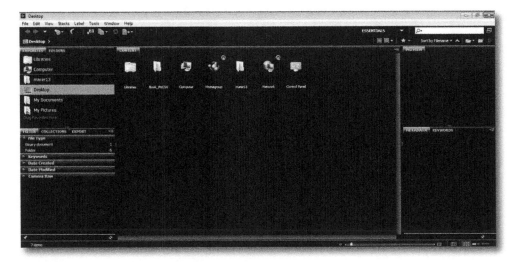

2 When Bridge opens open its Preferences using **Edit > Preferences...** on Windows or

Bridge > Preferences... on Mac.

In the Appearance section you have the options to change the colour of the interface like in Photoshop CS6.

3 Set the colour for the interface using one of the icons next to **Color Theme**.

4 You can change the default setting for colour by adjusting **User Interface Brightness** slider.

5 Use **Accent Color** drop-down menu to customise the colour that is being used for highlighting item that is selected (like Desktop link in this example):

Skip the rest of the General section for now. We only focus on certain preferences as there is not enough space to explain every single feature in this book. That's all you will need for now.

6 Click **OK** to accept the changes and close Bridge Preferences.

Now that you've customised what Bridge interface looks like, it is time to look around the interface and customise it. Bridge, like other Adobe applications, comes with a set of workspaces which change the visibility and positioning of panels within the application. The default workspace in Bridge is Essentials (like in Photoshop):

You can switch between workspaces using **Window > Workspace** menu:

You can also switch between Bridge workspaces using the workspace drop-down menu at the top of the application frame:

Now that you know how to switch between workspaces, let's look at ways to customise them.

7 Set your workspace to **Essentials**.

8 Reset your Essentials workspace to the default by choosing **Window > Workspace > Reset Workspace**.

Looking at Bridge interface (see screenshot at the beginning) there are three main sections within Bridge interface that can be resized:

• Left - Favorites, Folders, Filter, Collections and Export panels,

• Right - Preview, Metadata and Keywords panels,

• Centre - Content panel.

These three main sections can easily be resized by positioning the cursor on the edge between left side and centre or between right side and centre and dragging to resize the panels. You can also resize the panels vertically as much as horizontally. You just place the cursor between the panels, click and drag to resize the panels like this:

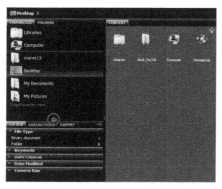

The same applies when resizing the panels between rights side and centre or left side and centre.

The central part of the Bridge interface - Content panel - displays the thumbnails of the files. The size of the thumbnails can be sized using the slider at the bottom of Bridge interface.

9 Using the slider at the bottom of Bridge interface increase or decrease the size of the thumbnails:

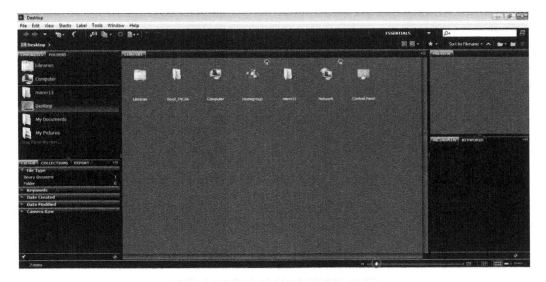

Note: You can also use keyboard shortcuts to increase the size of the thumbnails using Ctrl++/Cmd++ or decrease the size of the thumbnails using Ctrl+-/Cmd+-.

*Note 2: If your Content panel looks different, make sure that you have **View content as thumbnails** icon selected at the bottom right corner of Bridge interface (it's the default):*

All rights. Let's customise the Bridge interface. But first let's display some images.

10 Navigating inside the Folders panel on the left side of Bridge interface navigate to the location with some images on your hard drive.

11 Select one of the images inside Content panel (don't double-click because image will open in Photoshop).

With the image in Content panel selected notice how the preview of the image appears in **Preview** panel on the right side of Bridge interface. Because Preview is one of the panels, you can easily resize it and make it really big like I did here:

I'm actually going to show you another way to preview images, in full screen, so resize Preview panel back to its original size. You're going to love this tip!

12 With one of the images selected press **Spacebar** on your keyboard.

Spacebar launches full screen view and you can see the image without any distractions:

13 Now you can use the arrow keys on your keyboard to navigate between the images in full screen mode in Bridge!

14 To exit full screen view press Spacebar again or press **Escape** key.

Adobe Bridge can be used not just to preview images like JPEG, PNG, GIF or PSD but also any other file formats that Adobe applications can read.

The next screenshots shows Bridge opened with a PDF document selected:

Notice that this PDF file has two pages (page numbers in the Preview panel, below the preview) and you can browse through the pages using Adobe Bridge!

You don't even need to open the PDF in a PDF reader! That's a fantastic feature, don't you think? I think this is an amazing (one of many) feature in Bridge and I use it very often whenever I want to quickly find a document I'm looking for and I don't want to open every single document.

Another great feature in Bridge that I want to share with you is Slideshow feature.

Slideshow Mode

Slideshow mode in Bridge can be used for presenting a slideshow of images/files in full screen mode with images animating from one to another (fading in and fading out). It's a great feature to show others a collection of your images, especially if you connect your computer to a big screen or a projector.

15 Select the first image in a folder of images.

16 Choose **View > Slideshow**.

The slideshow starts and the images start fading in and out in a nice smooth way. Now let's customise the slideshow to give you a bit more control.

17 Exit the slideshow by pressing **Escape** key on your keyboard.

18 Choose **View > Slideshow Options...**

19 In **Slideshow Options** dialogue box set some options for your slideshow, like Slide Duration, Transition and how to Show Slides:

20 Click **Play** to accept the settings and run the slideshow again.

Now that you have some knowledge of Bridge and preview modes, it is time to look at some metadata and how to find it and use it using Adobe Bridge.

Metadata Panel

Here's the Metadata panel in all its glory:

What is Metadata? Metadata is a set of information about a file. Metadata includes information like file resolution, colour space, copyright, and many more. Digital cameras save some metadata information into the photos such as image dimensions, file format, the time the photo was taken, just to name a few.

How is Metadata stored? Metadata information is stored using a standard called **XMP** which stands for **EX**tensible **M**etadata **P**latform. XMP is built on XML language. XMP is also used when photos are edited with Camera Raw. XMP is great for exchanging information about files between different Adobe applications like Photoshop, Bridge and Illustrator, just to name a few.

325

XMP is also used for storing metadata for information like GPS location to make it easier to manage. One of the ways Adobe Bridge allows you to work with metadata is through the Metadata panel that you saw on the last screenshot. By default you will find it on the right side of your screen in Bridge.

Using Metadata panel you can view and edit the metadata of the file you have selected as well as perform searches for files.

Here's a description of main sections within the Metadata panel:

File Properties - it describes many properties of a file, including resolution, file size and colour profile among many others.

IPTC Core - it presents file's metadata that can be edited. IPTC specification was developed by International Press Telecommunications Council for professional news photography (photojournalism) and stock photography.

IPTC Extension - it includes additional information about photo content, like information about person and location shown in the photo.

Camera Data (Exif) - it presents information saved in a photo by a digital camera, including camera settings like aperture, shutter speed, and even camera and lens used:

GPS - information from a global positioning system (GPS) available in some digital cameras (and all mobile phones). If your camera doesn't have built-in GPS, there will be no GPS metadata here.

Camera Raw - settings applied by Camera Raw plug-in:

Audio - metadata for audio files like artist, album and track number.

Video - metadata for vide files like scene, shot and pixel aspect ratio.

DICOM - used in medicine, displays information saved in **D**igital **I**maging and **Co**mmunications in **M**edicine format.

Mobile SWF - metadata for SWF files, including author, title, description and copyright.

Finally, at the top of the Metadata panel you will find a section with some digital camera settings:

This section displays some very useful metadata information (especially useful for people interested in photography):

Columns from the left (from top to bottom):

- Aperture, Metering Mode, White balance,

- Shutter Speed, Exposure Compensation, ISO.

Aperture seems to be self-explanatory, however with **Metering Mode**, these are the descriptions of the icons (source: Adobe help):

⬚	Average or centerweighted average	⊙	Evaluative
⊡	Spot	⊡	Multispot
▦	Matrix or pattern	⊡	Partial
⊡	Centerweighted average or center weight	?	Other or unknown
ESP	Digital ESP		

and these are the descriptions of the icons for **White Balance**:

⊡	As shot	☀	Tungsten
AWB	Auto	≡	Fluorescent
☀	Daylight	⚡	Flash
☁	Cloudy	🛈	Custom
🏠	Shade		

In short, Metadata panel contains all you need to know about digital images.

What if you want to edit some metadata? Let's say you want to apply copyright to all your images? Here's what you do:

21 Select all the images you want to apply copyright to.

22 In Metadata panel, in IPTC Core section click on the drop-down menu next to

Copyright Status and choose **Copyrighted**:

23 Next, click the pencil icon next to **Copyright Notice** and type © **2013** followed by your name, e.g. © 2013 Marek Mularczyk.

24 Click away from the thumbnails and Bridge prompts you if you want to save the changes. Click **Apply** to save the changes.

Filters

That's not all when it comes to Metadata because you can also filter files using Metadata. Filter panel lets you filter files that appear in the Content area using a range of filters that we'll look at now.

You can fillter the view using all sorts of criteria.

25 Navigate to the Images folder in Bridge (or your own collection of images).

26 Open **Filter** panel (it appears on the left side of Bridge interface by default).

There are lots of different filters you can apply so I will give you just a few examples.

27 In the Filter panel expand a section callcd **Filc Type**.

If you're using Images folder that comes with this book, all images except one are JPEG files:

28 If you click JPEG file criteria only JPEGs in the folder will appear in the Content area.

29 Expand a section **Color Profile** and you'll see a number of different colour profiles:

30 Again by clicking one of the profiles you can quickly sort the files.

31 To remove the filter click on the filter again and this will display all the files.

All right, I think it is time to have a look at ways to bring images into Bridge from a memory card or straight from a camera connected to your computer. This will be a job for a Photo Downloader in Bridge.

Photo Downloader

This is one of these features that you wouldn't really think were possible with Bridge. Bridge is a file browser, some say. Yes, it is. But it is so much more. You can not only organise images with Bridge but also import images from your memory card or camera. You just plug in a memory card into a memory card reader or connect your camera with a usb cable and Bridge will detect it. Let's do it.

32 Plug in a memory card into a memory card reader or connect your camera to the computer running Bridge.

33 Open Bridge if you closed it.

34 In Bridge, click **Get Photos from Camera** button as shown here:

Note: You can also use File > Get Photos from Camera...

Photo Downloader will search for any memory cards or cameras connected to your computer and will display them. If you didn't connect a memory card or a camera you won't see any images in Photo Downloader. Photo Downloader is only for downloading images from digital cameras and memory cards. There is no option to download images from a location on a computer as Photo Downloader was not meant for that purpose.

This opens Photo Downloader:

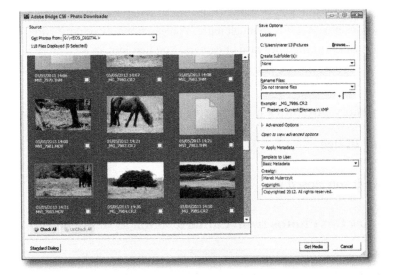

Note: If Photo Downloader is smaller and doesn't show previews of images, click Advanced Dialog button on the right side of the dialogue box.

35 On the left side of the window you can check only the images you want to import (I haven't checked any yet).

36 Moving to the right side of Photo Downloader choose the location where you want to save images:

Save Options

Location:

C:\Users\marer13\Pictures   Browse...

In the next section you can create a subfolder when copying images:

In this section I would choose **Custom Name** and type a name for a folder in the text field below.

37 Create a custom folder using one of the options on the drop-down menu that I have just described.

38 Moving to Advanced Options section tick the box next to **Save Copies to:** option:

This option allows you to create backups of photos you are importing. This is a fantastic feature because as you are importing photos from your memory card into your computer Photo Downloader can also create backups of all the photographs into another location such as an external drive. And it does it automatically! You don't need to manually copy photos onto another hard drive. Fabulous feature.

39 Click **Browse...** button to select a location where you want the backups to go.

40 Finally, expand **Apply Metadata** section if needed.

That's where you can apply copyright information to all photos you are importing:

41 From Template to Use drop-down menu choose **Basic Metadata**.

42 In **Creator** field type your name.

43 In the **Copyright** field type the copyright information, e.g. **Copyright 2013. All rights reserved**.

44 Now you can click **Get Media** to start downloading photos.

45 Once the photos finish downloading we'll add some labels and star rating in Bridge.

Star Rating and Labeling

When it comes to rating and labelling files, you have two options:

- you can label files with certain colour or

- apply rating of 0 to 5 stars.

Once you're done, you can sort files by their labels or star rating.

Note: You can label and rate not just files but also folders.

You can also add names to labels and the names will be added to file's metadata.

46 To apply labels to images, select one or more files in Bridge and choose one of the labels from **Label** menu.

Available options under **Label** menu are:

No Label, Select, Second, Approved, Review, To Do.

We're going to rate the image in this exercise as we can use rating later on in our Collections.

47 In Bridge, open the folder that you want to work with.

48 Select the first file in the Content area.

49 Look under Label menu and notice that you can use keyboard shortcuts **Ctrl/Cmd + 1 to 5** to add star rating to files.

The reason why I'm showing you how you can use the keyboard shortcuts is because you are going to apply star rating to files in full screen view. This will give you a chance to see the files previews big and you will be able to judge their quality and content when applying star rating.

50 With first file selected press **Spacebar** on your keyboard to enter full screen preview.

51 Apply a star rating to the file using **Ctrl/Cmd + 1 to 5**.

52 Navigate to the next file using the right arrow key on your keyboard and apply a star rating again.

53 Repeat steps for other files within the folder.

54 When done, press Escape to exit full screen view.

When you're done, you will see the files with star rating appear below them in the Content panel:

Collections

Collections can be used for grouping files in one place. If this sounds like something you could do with Explorer/Finder, what's amazing about Collections in Bridge is that the files can be located anywhere on your hard drive! The files can be spread across numerous folders in different locations.

There are two kinds of collections in Bridge:

- **Collections**,

- **Smart Collections**.

Collections are created manually by the user, while Smart Collections are automatic and are based on certain criteria.

Let's start with Collections first. Let's put them to practise.

55 Navigate to a folder with images and select some of them.

56 Open **Collections** panel (on the left side of Bridge interface).

57 With images selected click on **New Collection** icon in the bottom right corner of the

Collections panel:

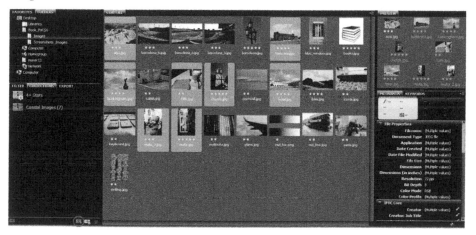

58 Bridge will display a dialogue box asking you if you want to include selected images in your collection. Click **Yes**:

59 Your new collection appears in the Collections panel and the name is highlighted. Name your collection.

Now your collection keeps the information about the location of images within the collection. If you want to add additional images to your collection, here's what you can do:

60 Navigate to another location on your computer where you have some files you would like to add to your collection.

61 Select the files you would like to add.

Note: Remember that you can use Ctrl on Windows / Cmd on Mac and click on any files you want to select to select multiple files at the same time. To select consecutive files hold Shift key down.

62 With the files selected drag and drop them onto the name of your collection in the Collections panel.

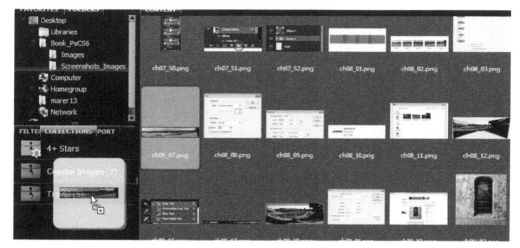

Collection updates and displays the number of files inside your collection.

What if you don't need an image in the collection anymore?

63 Click on the collection in the Collections panel.

64 Select a file you don't want in the collection anymore.

65 In the top right corner of the Content panel click **Remove from Collection** button:

This only removes the image from the collection, it doesn't remove the image from the hard drive or wherever you've downloaded the original images.

Here's a question I often get:

What if you have a file in your collection and you don't remember where the file is located on your computer? Can you somehow find it?

Yes, you can. Here's what you can do.

66 Select a file in your collection that you want to find.

67 Choose **File > Reveal in Bridge**.

Now it's time for **Smart Collections**.

Smart Collections are slightly different from collections as Smart Collections are based on certain criteria and are automatic meaning they update automatically whenever files meet these criteria. In this exercise, you are going to use star rating as criteria.

68 You don't need to select any files.

69 In the Collections panel click on New Smart Collection icon:

70 This will open **New Smart Collection** dialogue box as shown next.

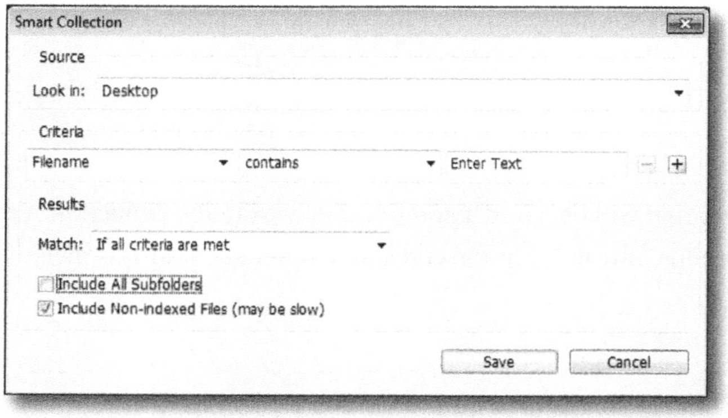

71 Click on the drop-down menu next to **Look in** to choose where you want Bridge search for files for your collection:

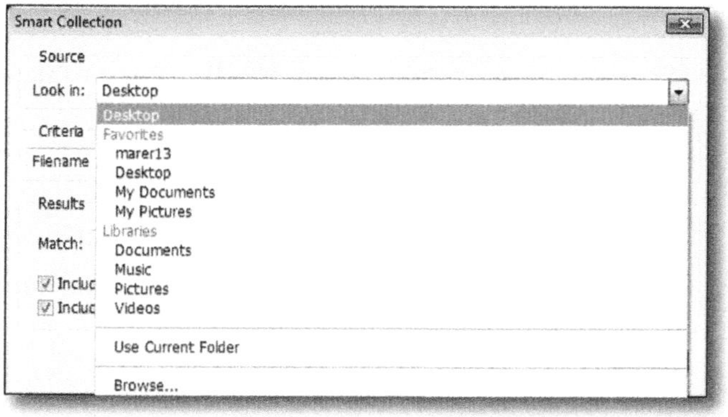

72 From the first Criteria drop-down menu choose what you want to use as a criteria for your collection. Choose **Rating**.

73 Next to Rating drop-down menu click on the next drop-down menu and choose **is greater than or equal to** and from the last one choose **4 stars**:

Now you have a criteria that will only add 4 and 5 star images to the collection. You can add additional criteria by clicking the plus button (+) at the end and another set of drop-down menus will appear:

There is a whole list of options available to you, including metadata like Copyright Notice, Color Mode, Focal Length, etc. In this case I'm fine with one so I'm going to click on the minus sign (-) next to second criteria to remove it.

Next is the **Results** section, where you can refine your smart collection, starting with Match drop-down menu.

74 Click on the **Match** drop-down menu in the Results section and choose **If all criteria are met**.

This option will make sure that if you have multiple criteria, the collection will only include images that match all criteria, not just one. In this case, you only have one, but leave it as **If all criteria are met** for future use.

Finally, you can choose whether you want to search all subfolders within the location you have chosen at the beginning or just the folder you have selected. I think it is best to check this option as you may have multiple subfolders within your destination (as we normally do).

75 Check **Include All Subfolders**.

Results

Match: If all criteria are met ▼

☑ Include All Subfolders
☑ Include Non-indexed Files (may be slow)

76 Click **Save** when done.

Bridge now creates your new Smart Collection and starts placing files inside the collection (files that match the criteria).

And here you go, here's how you work with Collections! Oh, one more thing. Remember that the Smart Collections are live. What do I mean by that? Well, if you add a new file anywhere inside the folder that Smart Collection is searching inside, and you give it 4 or 5 stars, the file will automatically appear inside your Smart Collection! But that's what you want, right? If you didn't, you would use a Collection not a Smart Collection. Let's give it a test to finish this part of the lesson.

77 Navigate anywhere inside the folder where Smart Collection is pointed.

78 Give some of the files 4 or 5 star rating.

79 In the Collections panel click the name of your Smart Collection.

80 When collection opens in the Content area, notice how it automatically updated!

This is one of great features of Smart Collections, they update automatically. I use Smart Collections for my best photographs. The moment I give a photo 4 or 5 star rating, I know it ends up in my Smart Collection straight away. When I want to upload my best photographs to my photography website, as an example, which you can find by the way at **mar-photos.com**, I just click on the name of the Smart Collection for my best photographs, select all photos in the Content panel and export them or open them in Photoshop if I need to resize them. Speaking of exporting, I just mentioned that, this is another great feature in Bridge/Photoshop that I'm going to show you at the end of the lesson.

On the other hand, you need to be a bit careful with Smart Collections. Here's why. Since your Smart Collection is automatic, it keeps updating without you knowing that. So if you change star rating of some of the files to say 2 or 3 stars, as an example, these files will be automatically removed from your collection.

Output to PDF

Adobe Bridge CS5 and CS6 lets you create PDF contact sheets and presentations (PDF slideshows). This feature is possible thanks to Adobe Output Module, which is a script that comes with Adobe Bridge CS5 and CS6. You can use Output Module to create PDF contact sheets or presentations as well as HTML/Flash web galleries (more on that in the next section of the lesson).

You can access the Output Module through the **Output workspace**.

In this part of the lesson you are going to create a PDF contact sheet with small thumbnails of multiple images on a sheet of paper (very popular with photographers for sharing thumbnails of photos with their clients so that clients can choose which photos they want).

81 Select the images you want to use in your contact sheet.

82 Change your workspace to Output using **Window > Workspace > Output**.

Here's the **Output workspace**:

83 Make sure that **PDF** button is selected in the Output panel at the top:

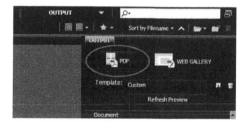

84 Once you've decided that you want to create a PDF click Template drop-down menu and choose **4*5 Contact Sheet** or **5*8 Contact Sheet** (depends how many images you have):

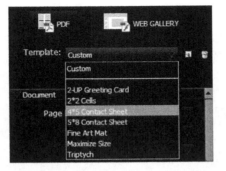

85 Click Refresh **Preview** button below to get a preview of the contact sheet.

Next section is a section called **Document**. In here, you can set what kind of document you're going to create (for print, for web) and set the dimensions for this document using a range of presets for web sizes as well as print sizes.

86 Click on **Page Preset** drop-down menu.

87 If you want to print your contact sheet choose **International Paper**, if you want to email it or show it on a computer/tablet screen choose **Web.**

Note: I've chosen Web as I'm going to display it on my tablet.

88 Once you've selected Page Preset, click **Size** drop-down menu and choose either **A4** (for

paper) or **1024 x 768** (for web):

*Note: If you're using Web preset, set the dimensions to the pixel dimensions of your device, i.e. I'm
going to change that to 1280 x 800 px.*

89 If you want to customise the dimensions as I mentioned above, change **Width** and

Height and keep Resolution (Quality) at **72 ppi**:

Directly below you can set the Quality. If you're not concerned about file size (if you're going to keep
it on your computer/tablet, set the Quality to maximum of 100. If you're going to email or upload the
contact sheet, set the Quality to 70-75.

90 Set the **Quality** as mentioned above.

91 Next you can set the Background colour. You can either choose the colour from the drop-down menu or you can click on the colour swatch next to it:

Below, you will find two fields for Open Password and Permission Password:

Open Password - you can add a password and the user will need to type in a password to open PDF,

Permission Password - this is one of my favourites, you can add a permission password so the user won't be able to print PDF if you tick Permission Password and Disable Printing.

Note: If you want to use both Open Password and Permission Password, you will need to use different passwords for these options.

92 Tick **Open Password** if you want to protect your PDF from being used without your knowledge. Enter password.

93 Tick **Permission Password** and **Disable Printing** if you want to protect your PDF from being printed. Enter password.

The next section is called **Layout**. In this section you can change number of rows or columns if needed. As I have 19 photographs selected, 4*5 layout is fine so I'm not going to change it.

Another option in this section is the margins. You can change margins and make thumbnails smaller (or bigger). By default Photoshop sets **margins** to **12 px** each side.

94 Change number of columns or margins if needed.

Overlays section is next.

95 Make sure **Filename** is ticked and untick **Extension**.

Filename is great for contact sheets as your client will see the names of the files below the thumbnails and they can tell you which photos they want/like. They don't need to see the file extensions, that's why we've unticked them.

96 Below Filename you can choose what **Font, Size** and **Color** you want to use for your

text below the thumbnails:

97 Skip **Page Number** as we won't need them unless you have loads of images selected.

Next two sections are **Header** and **Footer** where you can add some text at the top and the bottom of the page. We're going to add some branding on the top and copyright information at the bottom of the page. And again, you'll be able to fully customise the font used in the Header and Footer.

98 Check **Add Header** in the Header section and set the drop-down menu next to it to Left, Right or Center.

99 In text field below, next to **Text**, type your name or your company's name and customise text properties such as Font, Size and Color:

Note: As you're increasing text size, you will need to increase Distance and Bridge will notify you about that when you click Refresh Preview button:

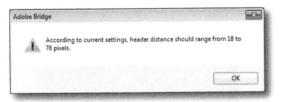

100 Adjust the **Distance** if notified by Bridge.

101 You can also add a **Divider** - a horizontal line separating the header from the content.

For Footer, you will add the copyright information.

102 Tick **Add Footer** and set the alignment to **Center**.

103 In the text field next to Text type ©**2013** followed by your name and then type **All rights reserved.**

103 Set font properties like you did with the header but this time set text to be very small:

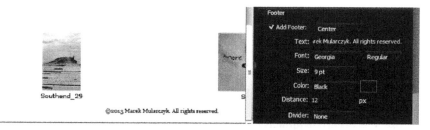

104 Skip **Playback** section (unless you want to create a multipage presentation)

105 Check **View PDF After Save** and click **Save...** button. Give your PDF a name and save it.

Here you go. You're done with a PDF contact sheet. If you checked View PDF After Save option, you will now see the PDF open in your PDF reader and you may be asked for a password:

106 If prompted, type the password to open your PDF contact sheet.

Well done, you have created a PDF contact sheet using Adobe Bridge. Now it's time for the last part of this lesson - exporting files using Image Processor.

File Export with Image Processor

Image Processor can be used for converting and batch processing large numbers of files, i.e. when you want to quickly export the whole folder of images and maybe even convert them to another file format. Unlike the Batch command, the **Image Processor** lets you process files without first creating an action.

Here are some things that are possible with **Image Processor**:

- you can convert files to JPEG, PSD or TIFF formats (or all of them at the same time),

- you can resize files to certain dimensions,

- you can convert images to sRGB colour space, and

- you can add copyright information to the files.

- you can even run an Action.

Let's put it in practise.

107 Open Bridge if you closed it and navigate to the folder with files that you want to export.

108 Select all the images.

109 Choose **Tools > Photoshop > Image Processor...**

Image Processor will open in Photoshop. Here's the **Image Processor**:

110 In **Step 1** Photoshop is already using the files you selected in Bridge so you can leave it as it is.

111 In **Step 2** you need to choose a location for the export. You can leave it as **Save in Same Location**.

Leaving Step 2 as Save in Same Location is fine as Photoshop will create a subfolder in the same location with the name of the file format that you're going to use. Don't worry, Photoshop will not overwrite the original images.

If, however, you prefer to save the exported image somewhere else, you can choose the other option and choose a folder.

112 Step number **3 - File Type**. Choose the file format you want to use. I'm going to choose JPEG as an example:

113 If you've chosen JPEG as well, set **Quality** (Highest: 10 to 12, High: 8 to 9).

114 If you're exporting images to the web (websites, social networks, email), check **Convert Profile to sRGB**.

115 You can also resize images to certain dimensions (**W** and **H** on the right hand side).

Note: As you may have noticed I set my W and H to 800 px each. This is not going to make images square. The way it works is Photoshop will take the longer side of the image and resize it to match the value. The image will retain its original proportions.

116 The last section is **Preferences**:

Preferences

☐ Run Action: Default Actions | Vignette (selection)

Copyright Info: Marek Mularczyk 2013 Copyrighted. All rights reserv

☑ Include ICC Profile

117 Make sure that **Include ICC Profile** is checked. This will embed the colour profile within the images.

118 Next to **Copyright Info:** type your copyright information and Photoshop will embed it within each image.

119 When done, you just click **Run** in the top right hand corner.

Now Photoshop will do all the magic. It will open every single image, resize it (if required), save it and close it. And it works as easily on ten images as on a hundred images.

Image Processor in Photoshop

Image Processor is a Photoshop feature as you noticed. We started it from Bridge but you can open it directly in Photoshop as well.

If you want to run Image Processor from within Photoshop, in Photoshop choose **File > Script > Image Processor...**

This opens exactly the same dialogue box, with one difference. If you open Image Processor from within Photoshop, without selecting any images like you did in Bridge, when Image Processor opens, in Step 1 you will need to do one of the following:

- check **Use Open Images** (if you opened images in Photoshop), or

- click **Select Folder** button and select a folder with images.

And that's all there is to it. That's how you can easily take a folder of images and quickly export it to one of three image file formats and Photoshop will do all the work for you.

You're done! Congratulations! One more lesson finished. There is one more final lesson left.

In the last lesson, you're going to explore the world of Adobe Camera Raw.

Lesson 12

Adobe Camera Raw

In this last lesson, you are going to explore Adobe Camera Raw and learn things like:

*   Raw Files and Camera Raw

*   Exploring Camera Raw

*   Cropping and Straightening Images

*   Developing Photos Non-Destructively

*   Creating Lens Vignetting

*   Applying a Graduated Filter

*   Clearing and Applying Camera Raw Settings

*   Radial Filter in Camera Raw 8 (New in Photoshop CC)

*   Spot Removal in Camera Raw 8 (New Features in Photoshop CC)

Raw files

You are probably familiar with JPEG file format, maybe not with raw. You could say that raw is just another file format, but it's so much more than that. Raw is an amazing file format. Think of raw as your digital negative. You can develop (process) a raw file at any time without loosing the quality and working non-destructively. When you edit a raw file, the original raw data is being preserved. That's why all edits to raw files are non-destructive.

So where are the edits stored?

Edits to raw files can be kept:

- in a sidebar file (.xmp file),

- in a database (i.e. in Adobe Photoshop Lightroom),

- in the file itself (.dng file).

Why would you want to take photographs in raw and not in JPEG?

When you take photos in JPEG, the files are compressed and adjusted by the camera. You have very little control over what camera does to your JPEGs. Not the same with raw. Raw files are uncompressed and unedited raw files straight from the camera. Raw files capture everything from the scene you are photographing without applying any compression. Photographing in raw lets you make all sorts of changes to things like white balance, as an example.

Is shooting raw better than shooting JPEGs? Does raw offer better image quality?

Yes and yes to both questions. Only raw gives you the highest possible quality. However, keep in mind that raw files are bigger than JPEGs (obviously since they contain more information than JPEGs which are compressed. Raw is not just about the file size and no compression. When shooting raw you don't need to worry about the colour space or the white balance as these can easily be changed inside Camera Raw. I often use an analogy to compare raw vs JPEG and I explain that shooting JPEG is like taking photographs on film, developing them and throwing away the film. What you're left with are prints.

Is raw file a file with a .raw file extension?

Yes and no. There is a raw file format with a .raw file extension but this is just one of many raw file formats. The only disadvantage, if we can call that a disadvantage, is that there are many raw file formats. Every camera manufacturer has its own proprietary raw file format.

Here's something for you. Look at this image:

.3fr	Hasselblad	.dcr	Kodak	.orf	Olympus
.arw	Sony	.drf	Kodak	.ptx	Pentax
.srf	Sony	.k25	Kodak	.pef	Pentax
.sr2	Sony	.kdc	Kodak	.pxn	Logitech
.bay	Casio	.tif	Kodak	.r3d	Red
.crw	Canon	.erf	Epson	.raf	Fuji
.cr2	Canon	.fff	Imacon	.raw	Panasonic
.cap	Phase One	.mef	Mamiya	.rw2	Panasonic
.tif	Phase One	.mos	Leaf	.raw	Leica
.iiq	Phase One	.mrw	Minolta	.rwl	Leica
.eip	Phase One	.nef	Nikon	.rwz	Rawzor
.dcs	Kodak	.nrw	Nikon	.x3f	Sigma

This image shows all different raw file formats from all major camera manufacturers. If you look closer you will notice that even the same manufacturer may have more than raw file format, i.e. Canon has **.crw** (old one) and **.cr2** (new one).

The good news is **Camera Raw** supports all major raw file formats and cameras. The list of cameras that are supported by Camera Raw is almost endless so instead of listing the cameras that Camera Raw supports, I will give you a link instead.

You can find a list of all supported cameras here:

http://www.adobe.com/go/learn_ps_cameraraw

On this list you can also find out if your camera can save photos as raw (every SLR camera does and some compact cameras do, but not many of them).

Now that you know about raw files, we'll have a look at Adobe Camera Raw. I'll explain what it is and how it works. And how to use it.

Adobe Camera Raw

Adobe Camera Raw (ACR) is a plug-in that comes with Photoshop and Bridge. I still remember the times when Camera Raw could only process raw files, but not any more. Camera Raw was created for developing raw images from digital cameras but nowadays you can also process JPEGs and TIFFs in Camera Raw. Camera Raw supports images up to 65,000 px on the longer side and up to 512 megapixels. When you use Camera Raw for editing images, all the changes are stored in a sidecar file with .xmp file extension and the original data is preserved. What it means is that Camera Raw lets you work non-destructively and the pixels within the image are not altered.

Camera Raw is a free plug-in that comes with Photoshop and Bridge and cannot be purchased or downloaded separately. All updates to Camera Raw are free and they bring support for newer cameras and lenses as well as bug fixes and security improvements.

In the recent years Camera Raw became much more sophisticated than it used to be. Nowadays, Camera Raw lets you perform some of the operations that used to be possible only inside Photoshop. This doesn't mean that Camera Raw replaces Photoshop. Not at all. Camera Raw is just a step in process of developing photographs

Let's get started.

Note: Because of the file size of raw files, in this lesson you will either need to use your own raw images or use JPEGs if you don't have any raw files.

1 Open Bridge and navigate to the folder with images you're going to edit with Camera Raw.

2 Select one of the images that you want to edit, right-click on it and choose **Open in Camera Raw...**

Note: If you double-click on a raw file in Bridge, the file will open in Camera Raw but in Photoshop. By right-clicking on the raw file you can open it in Camera Raw in Bridge without opening Photoshop.

Here's an image opened in Camera Raw:

Note: If you open more than one image in Camera Raw, you will see a filmstrip with images on the right hand side.

Camera Raw dialogue box displays a big preview of the image in the centre.

In the upper right hand corner there is a histogram showing the tonal range of the image.

*Note: The RGB histogram that appears in the upper right hand corner is based on the output space in the **Workflow Options**, which I will explain in just a moment.*

In the centre at the bottom you can see your workflow options. You're going to change them in just a moment.

On the top there is a range of tools for zooming, panning, as well as adjusting images.

On the right hand side there is a group of panels with tabs representing different options for adjusting images. That's where you will be spending most of your time when editing images.

The best practise for editing images with Camera Raw is to move from left to right and from top to bottom. You're going to explore all the options as you start editing the image.

Workflow Options that you're going to set up now is something you only do one and then Camera Raw will remember that.

3 Click on the link for **Workflow Options**:

4 **Workflow Options** dialogue box opens:

Space should be set to match your color space in Photoshop.

5 Set Depth to **16 Bits/Channel**.

Note: 16 Bits/Channel will let you use maximum number of levels within the images.

6 **Size** lets you open images in smaller or larger dimensions. Leave it on the default - original size (the one without plus or minus sign).

7 **Resolution** - set it to **300 ppi**.

Note: Resolution here has no impact on the pixel dimensions of the images.

8 Leave **Sharpen For:** set to **None** as you will sharpen the images yourself.

9 Click **OK**.

From now on, Camera Raw will remember your Workflow Options so you don't need to worry about them anymore.

Back to the main Camera Raw window, let's look at how you can view/navigate images inside Camera Raw.

Bottom left corner of Camera Raw contains buttons for zoomin in and out as well as a drop-down menu which you can use to choose magnification:

Alternatively, you can use Zoom tool in the upper left corner of Camera Raw:

With Zoom tool selected you can click on the image to zoom in and if you hold **Alt** key down and click you can zoom out.

Let's start with some cropping and straightening in Camera Raw and then we'll proceed to developing the image.

Cropping and Straightening in Camera Raw

Before you open the image in Photoshop, you can crop it in Camera Raw. You can also use Straighten tool in Camera Raw to straighten the image. Let's have a look at the Crop tool.

10 Select Crop tool from the tools in the top left corner of Camera Raw:

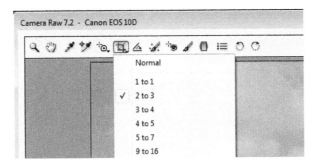

11 If you click and hold on Crop tool, you'll see a list of crop presets available:

Presets on this drop-down menu are presets for certain aspect ratios, not pixel dimensions.

Here's what I would do:

12 Just select Crop tool and click and drag over the entire image.

13 Now if you want to crop the image, but keep the aspect ratio of the image, hold **Shift** key down and start dragging from one of the corners:

Dragging from a corner handle with Shift key held down keeps the original aspect ratio of the image.

14 Once you've defined the crop, double-click inside the crop area.

Next, let's straighten the image.

15 Select **Straighten tool** from the tools on the top:

16 With Straighten tool click and drag along a line that's supposed to be a straight horizontal line within the image, like a bottom of the building for example:

17 When you release the mouse button, you will see an overlay of the crop preview and you just double-click inside the crop overlay to crop the image.

Now that you've managed to crop and straighten the image, let's do some photo development. So now we're going to move to the right side of the Camera Raw dialogue box.

Basic panel

You're now going to use the Basic panel to perform main tonal and colour adjustments. With most images, Basic panel may be enough to make images look better.

Here's the **Basic panel**:

Let's start with **White Balance**:

White Balance reflects the colour temperature of the lighting conditions when a photograph was taken. If you photograph in raw you don't have to worry about white balance as you can set it in Camera Raw. By default, when you open an image in Camera Raw, White Balance will be set to **As Shot** (as you can see from the screenshots above) which is the white balance that was embedded in a photo by the camera.

18 Start by going through different **White Balance** settings to find the one that looks best on the photo you have opened.

19 If there's still any magenta or green colour tint in the image, use **Tint** slider to adjust it:

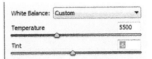

Next, **Exposure**

Use Exposure slider to brighten the image, focusing on the midtones (for highlights you will use Highlights and Whites sliders).

20 Start dragging **Exposure** slider if your image is too bright or too dark.

Note: Be careful, don't move the Exposure slider too far to the right as the image will start losing the details. Also, notice how the histogram updates as you're moving the Exposure slider.

Contrast

Adobe made some changes to Contrast and now it so much better than it used to be. Contrast is now adapting to what the image content is. Contrast slider will adjust the contrast on the midtones, which you adjusted with Exposure slider. Exposure and Contrast are these two sliders that should make your image look much better and then it's just a matter of fine-tuning the image.

21 Adjust the contrast in the image using the **Contrast** slider (I increased it to 38 as shown on the screenshot above).

Highlights and **Shadows**

Contrast	+38
Highlights	0
Shadows	0

After you have adjusted Exposure and Contrast, it is time for Highlights and Shadows. Using these sliders you can work on highlights and shadows separately, without affecting the midtones.

22 Adjust **Highlights** and **Shadows** within the image using the corresponding sliders.

Note: If you want to see any Highlights or Shadows clipping, hold Alt key down as you're dragging the sliders. This also works for other adjustments in Camera Raw.

Whites and **Blacks**

Shadows	0
Whites	0
Blacks	0

Using the previous four sliders, you should have achieved a very well toned image. However, you could potentially used Whites and Blacks sliders to adjust the extremes of the Highlights and Shadows. You wouldn't be using these two sliders on every image, though.

23 If needed, adjust **Whites** and **Blacks**.

In my example, I used Blacks to fine-tune the darkest areas within the image:

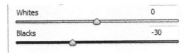

Just to repeat what you have done so far, just so you remember that, this is the order in which you will be editing images in the Basic panel:

- You start with the Exposure and then the Contrast.

- Once you've adjusted these, Highlights and Shadows.

- In many cases, this will be enough. If not, use Whites and Blacks to adjust the extremes of the Highlights and Shadows.

When adjusting the highlights and shadows in your images, be careful not to loose the details in either shadows or highlights (especially when trying to make highlights much brighter). This may become more apparent when you print images, not that much with images on your computer' or tablet' screen.

Also remember that most images won't need Blacks adjustments (especially not dragging the Blacks slider to the right). However, some images will actually benefit from black clipping, as it's called, basically moving the Blacks slider to the left, sometimes quite a lot.

Here's an example where the image benefits from quite large Blacks adjustment:

Let's move on. There are three more sliders in the Basic panel left.

Clarity

Clarity seems a bit like contrast and many people think of clarity like another 'contrast slider'. However, clarity actually works on increasing contrast in the midtones. As you increase the clarity value (as you move the slider to the right), you are applying clarity to wider regions within the photograph. All your photographs will benefit from some clarity (the only situation when I don't use clarity or use it just a little bit is with portraits to keep them quite soft in the midtones).

24 Add **Clarity** if needed (I added around +54):

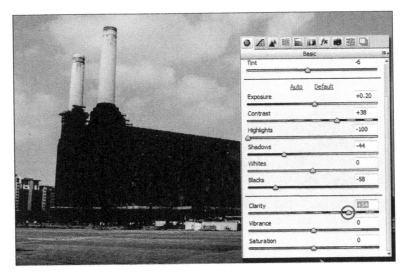

Note: You can also add negative value to clarity to soften the image even more (I use that sometimes for portraits).

Vibrance and **Saturation**

Vibrance and Saturation may seem to be the same to many users, but they're really not. They do both increase the saturation, that's true. However, while Saturation increases the saturation of all the colours within the image, Vibrance protects the colours that are saturated already and only increases the saturation of the colours that are not saturated already. Vibrance also protects skin tones, while Saturation doesn't.

25 If you have, open an image of a landscape or flowers and try increasing value for both Saturation and Vibrance sliders to see the difference.

With the image I have opened, Im going to slightly increase Vibrance to boos the saturation of the colours that are not saturated already. This will increase the saturation of the sky and the grass in front of the building.

And that's the Basic panel. If that's what you wanted to do with the image, you could now:

- click **Open** button to open the image in Photoshop and do some more work on it, or

- you could click **Save Image...** to save it as a JPEG or PSD file, or

- you could click **Done** to close Camera Raw with all the edits remembered:

| Save Image | | ProPhoto RGB; 16 bit; 2314 by 1876 (3.3MP); 300 ppi | | Open Copy | Reset | Done |

Now, you're going to move to the next panel - **Tone Curve** panel.

Tone Curve panel

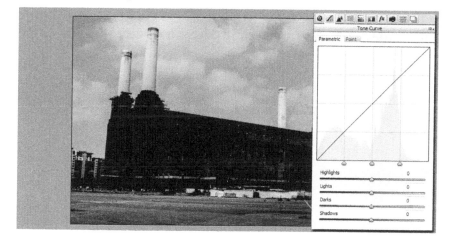

In addition to what you have done to adjust the image already, you can use Tone Curve panel to fine-tune it even more in terms of contrast. There are two modes within the Tone Curve: Parametric and Point (you can see them at the top of the Tone Curve panel).

Parametric mode is what you see when you navigate to the Tone Curve panel. To edit the tone curve, which you can see, you use the sliders below the curve.

Note: You can use the Target Adjustment tool when using the Tone Curve panel (like in Curves in Photoshop):

Note: You can see me using screenshots in Camera Raw 7, which is the version shipping wth Photoshop CS6. I will show you something new in Camera Raw 8, which ships with Photoshop CC later in this lesson. Because most feature are the same, I will keep using screenshots from Camera Raw 7.

In **Point mode** you can use the Tone Curve like you use Curves in Photoshop, by clicking and dragging on the curve. Or you can use **Curve** drop-down menu and choose one of the presets to add more contrast to the image.

26 Add more contrast, if needed, using one of the methods described above.

Detail panel

Detail panel is used for sharpening images (and more). In the past, sharpening would typically be done inside Photoshop but now as sharpening in Camera Raw is so much better than it used to be in the past, you will be sharpening images in Camera Raw as you adjust them going through the panels.

Sharpening section within the Detail panel consists of four sliders: Amount, Radius, Detail and Masking. The settings you see on the screenshot above are the default settings that Camera Raw uses when you open an image and navigate to the Detail panel.

Note: If you open a JPEG or a TIFF file, the sliders will be set to 0% for each.

The two main controls here are: **Amount** and **Radius**. These two sliders control how much sharpening is being applied to the image and how the sharpening is being applied.

27 First set the image magnification to **100%** (as advised at the bottom of the Detail panel).

28 Start increasing the Amount setting and notice how the image becomes sharper.

29 Once you've set the Amount, you're going to use the **Radius** slider.

Radius in here works in exactly the same way as the Radius slider inside Unsharp Mask or Smart Sharpen in Photoshop. You can use a lower value to sharpen fine detail in the image, or you can use a higher value to apply sharpening to wider edges within the image. For most images, you would typically use values around 1.0 for the Radius.

*Note: You can see how sharpening is being applied to the edges within the image by holding down **Alt** key as you're dragging the **Radius** slider:*

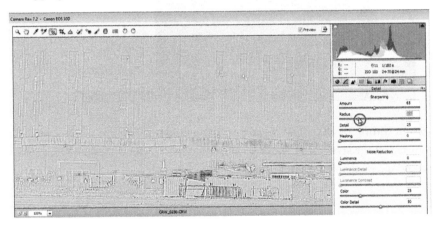

Amount and Radius sliders control sharpening of the image and you've done it. So if you're wondering what Detail and Masking are doing here, you're going to find out now.

Detail and **Masking**

Once you've sharpened the image, you can use Detail slider to fine-tune the sharpening without creating too much of a 'halo effect' around the edges.

30 Adjust **Detail** slider to fine-tune sharpening.

*Note: To see exactly what's happening hold **Alt** key down as you're dragging the slider.*

When it comes to **Masking**, you can use this slider to apply more sharpening to the edges than to the entire image. As you adjust the Masking slider, a mask is being created. If you hold Alt key down on your keyboard as you're dragging the slider, you will initially see the white mask overlay (everything should turn white if your masking is set to 0). As you start dragging the slider, more and more areas within the mask become black. White represents areas where sharpening is not being masked, and black represents areas where sharpening is being masked. In other words, as you change Masking slider, white shows you which areas within the image are being sharpened.

31 Adjust Masking slider to define which areas within the image should be sharpened.

32 You can zoom out on the image as you won't need 100% anymore.

We'll skip Noise Reduction and we'll move on to the next panel - **HSL / Grayscale**.

HSL / Grayscale panel

As you may have guessed already, **HSL / Grayscale panel** lets you convert images to black and white (the Grayscale bit), but what about this HSL bit? HSL stands for Hue, Saturation and Lightness, to start with. Now that you know that, you probably may guess that HSL will work like a Hue and Saturation adjustment in Photoshop. And you wouldn't be wrong about that. However, HSL panel is more powerful than just a Hue and Saturation panel in Photoshop.

Just look at the controls here:

You've got three tabs: Hue, Saturation and Luminance, and each of the tabs contains eight controls for different colours within the image. Let's put it in practise.

33 Using Camera Raw open **buckingham.jpg** from the Images folder.

34 In HSL / Grayscale panel navigate to the **Luminance** tab and take **Blues** slider all the way to the left:

Now you can see the power of the HSL panel in action! The sky looks fantastic! Maybe a bit too saturated, but you get the idea. Now, let's increase the colours on the statue. Let's make it really look golden.

35 Navigate to the **Saturation** tab and take **Yellows** all the way to the right.

If you want to make a beautiful black and white image instead, here's what you can do (with the same photograph).

36 Undo the last few steps with **Luminance** and **Saturation**.

Note: I almost forgot to give you a precious tip. If you want to move the sliders to their original positions and you don't remember what their original positions are (who does?), just double-click on the sliders. This will move them back to their original positions whatever they were.

37 Check **Convert to Grayscale** at the top of the panel:

38 Now the tabs change to just one tab: **Grayscale Mix**. Now you can use the **Blues** and

Yellows sliders to play with the sky and the statue:

39 Experiment with the sliders and when done, click **Done** button and reopen the image

you were working on earlier.

Just before we move on to the next section, I want to show you another great technique using
HSL / Grayscale. You're going to love it, trust me!

40 From the Images folder open **ibiza.jpg** in Camera Raw.

Note: Remember that everything you're doing in Camera Raw is non-destructive and can easily be reversed at any time (I will show you how to do it near the end of the chapter).

41 Navigate to the **HSL / Grayscale** panel.

42 Open **Saturation** tab.

43 Drag **Oranges**, **Yellows** and **Greens** sliders all the way to the left:

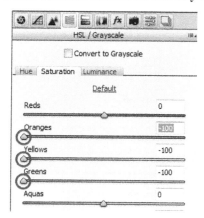

Now, what you get is a beautiful black and white photograph with the car in colour! Isn't it great? I think it's a fantastic design idea. It reminds me a very popular effect where you have a black and white image of a bride with a red rose. Exactly the same effect you have here:

It's time to move on. We're going to skip Split Toning and we'll move on to **Lens Corrections**.

44 You can close the photo of the car and open any image you want.

Lens Corrections

Lens Corrections panel helps deal with any lens distortions within images. It fixes many of the common faults/distortions. To work efficiently, Lens Correction filter needs to access EXIF data from the camera to detect what camera and lens were used for capturing a photo so that it can find a matching lens profile to deal with the distortions.

45 With the image you have open inside Camera Raw, check the box next to **Enable Lens Profile Corrections**.

Camera Raw will try to find a matching profile that matches the lens that was used. In my case, it found a matching profile for one of the Canon lenses I used - Canon EF-S 17-85mm f/4-5.6:

If using automatic profile doesn't work (or if Camera Raw didn't detect the lens that was used), you could choose a lens that you used from the **Model** drop-down menu. Or, if this doesn't work, you can switch to **Manual** mode:

In Manual mode, you can manually remove geometric distortions as well as any horizontal or vertical distortions, using the sliders provided.

At the bottom, in the Manual mode, you will see another section called **Lens Vignetting**.

Lens Vignetting is an effect of darkening or brightening the edges of photographs, mainly found on wide angle lenses. Amount slider in the Lens Vignetting section can be used to reduce lens vignetting effect on the photographs.

Note: Lens Vignetting in Camera Raw was originally meant for reducing lens vignetting in the photographs, but I have some friends who actually create lens vignetting effects on their photographs!

Effects

As I mentioned earlier, some photographers started creating lens vignetting effects instead of removing vignettes from their images. And that's where Effects panel comes in. You can create vignettes in the Lens Corrections panel. However, lens vignetting within the Lens Corrections panel only applies to the entire image. What if you cropped the image? That's where **Post Crop Vignetting** inside the Effects panel comes in:

For example, the image that I have been working on earlier in this chapter, was cropped:

So in this case, I'm going to use the Effects panel and the **Post Crop Vignetting** section.

46 If you cropped the image you were working on earlier in this lesson, you can follow along. Reopen it in Camera Raw.

47 Navigate to the **Effects** panel.

48 In the **Post Crop Vignetting** section decrease the **Amount** to start with:

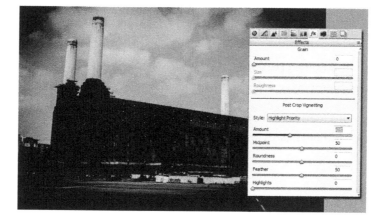

Let me explain the option.

Post Crop Vignetting options:

- **Amount** - it is the amount of darkening or lightening that will occur in the Post Crop Vignette.

- **Midpoint** - this slider moves the effect towards the center or toward the corner of the image.

- **Roundness** - this controls how round or oval the resulting effect is.

- **Feather** - this controls how hard or soft the effect will gradate in and out.

- **Highlights** - it allows to increase the highlight contrast in the areas that are vignetted.

Note: Highlights slider is initially disabled and it will only become available when you move the Amount slider to the left.

49 Adjust the sliders to your liking to get the desired effect.

Post Crop Vignetting styles:

- **Highlight Priority** - it tends to create more dramatic results.

- **Color Priority** - it preserves the colour appearance while making the corners darker. It seems to maintain the colour purity very well and is most often used.

- **Paint Overlay** - this used to be the default and only choice in older versions of Camera Raw. It darkens the image without regard to its contents.

Grain effect

At the top of the Effects panel there is one more section called **Grain**. It was created by the Adobe team to recreate the film grain effect on digital images. Here's what the sliders do:

- **Amount** - it determines how much grain you're adding to the image.

- **Size** - it controls the size of the grain. Larger grain sizes may soften your image.

- **Roughness** - it controls how regular the grain is. Moving slider to the right makes grain more irregular.

50 Experiment with the grain effect if you want and then move on to the next panel.

Tip: You can access panels in Camera Raw using keyboard shortcuts:

Ctrl+Alt+Number (0 to 9) on Windows

Cmd+Opt+Number (0 to 9) on Mac.

Camera Calibration panel

Camera Calibration panel allows you to choose which Process Version you want to use when a raw file is being rendered inside Camera Raw, with 2012 being the latest one. There have been many changes to the way raw image have been processed in Camera Raw and Process Version has been growing with new releases of Camera Raw. Process Version 2012 brings lots of new features and improvement, which I am not going to go into detail about in here. When you edit a photo that was edited in earlier versions of Camera Raw using either a Process 2003 or a Process 2010, you will see an exclamation mark in the bottom right corner of the preview. Clicking on this icon will update the Process Version to 2012, which will allow you to work with the latest features in Camera Raw processing.

The **Camera Profile** dropdown menu displays the version of Camera Raw used when the camera was first profiled as well as subsequent updates and the new DNG Profiles for the camera. It also lists profiles trying to match camera vendors settings like Landscape, Portrait, etc. The list will depend on the file you opened as there are separate profiles for Canon and Nikon and others. Here's the list for Canon , as an example:

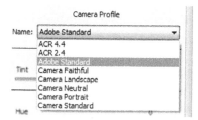

Adobe Standard represents the default camera vendors settings for main cameras supported by Camera Raw. Using Adobe Standard you should get a very good rendering of the defaults from your camera. So what it means to you is that if you set Camera Profile to Adobe Standard, Camera Raw will render the image in the same way as Canon's or Nikon's software does. And normally, you just leave it as it is.

51 Leave all the controls as they are. Make sure that Process is set to **2012** and Camera Profile to **Adobe Standard**:

52 Click Done or Save Image once you've finished.

Graduated Filter tool

This is the last part of the lesson and we're approaching the end of the book. There are a number of tools inside Camera Raw and it would take many many pages to describe them all. So I thought I would show you one of them to give you an idea how you can work with tools non-destructively inside Camera Raw. The one I've picked up is the Graduated Filter tool.

The **Graduated Filter** is a tool that helps photographers create correct exposure and is a very nice addition to Camera Raw tools. Graduated Filter can be used to apply local adjustments to specific areas of images. Graduated Filter can be used to make a number of adjustments, including Exposure, Contrast, Brightness, Clarity and many more. Typically, the way it's being used, is for darkening bright areas of the sky or brightening dark areas of the foreground.

Here are the controls available for the Graduated Filter:

53 Open an image of a landscape (or ibiza.jpg).

54 Select the **Graduated Filter** tool from the tools at the top of Camera Raw:

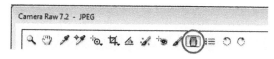

55 On the right side of Camera Raw start by lowering the Exposure to about **-1**:

56 Click at the top of the image, hold the mouse button down and drag towards the line of the horizon:

57 Once you release the mouse button, you will start adjusting the settings.

58 Adjust the **Exposure**.

With this image, I'm going to set the Exposure to -1.5.

59 Try changing other properties like Contrast and notice how the sky changes.

The Graduated Filter tool is an amazing addition to Camera Raw. In this example here, I've managed to recover the details in the sky. That was the original sky but the camera didn't seem to register everything as they often do because of the lightness differences between the sky and the foreground.

60 If you want to reposition the filter, click on the bottom pin and drag:

61 If you want to rotate the filter, position the cursor on the line on the side of the pin and when it changes to two arrows, click and drag:

And that's how the Graduated Filter tool works inside Camera Raw. Keep experimenting with the tool and its settings. Keep exploring. And remember, you can add additional graduated filters using the New button on the right side.

62 Click Done when finished to exit Camera Raw.

There's one more final technique that I want to share with you. You have made some adjustments to images inside Camera Raw and you've exported images from Camera Raw as well. What if you want to reverse what you've done? What if you don't like the effect and you want to take the image back to its original state? That's what I'm going to show you in this last bit of this lesson.

Clearing and Applying Camera Raw settings

First, let's start with looking at images you edited with Camera Raw.

63 Open Adobe Bridge if it's not already running.

64 Navigate to the folder with images you edited in Camera Raw.

Notice that images that were edited with Camera Raw have this icon in the top right corner:

Note: Next to the 'edited' icon there is another one that represents crop, because this image was cropped inside Camera Raw as well.

I'm going to show you something very interesting next. You've done some editing to one of the images (I'm going to use the image of the Battersea Power Station in London as an example) and you want to edit some other images in the same way. Here's what you can do.

65 Reopen the image you were working on in Camera Raw.

66 Navigate to the **Presets** panel:

67 Click the **New Preset** icon at the bottom of the panel (the icon looks like a page icon and it's next to the bin icon).

68 **New Preset** dialogue box opens where you can choose which presets you want to save:

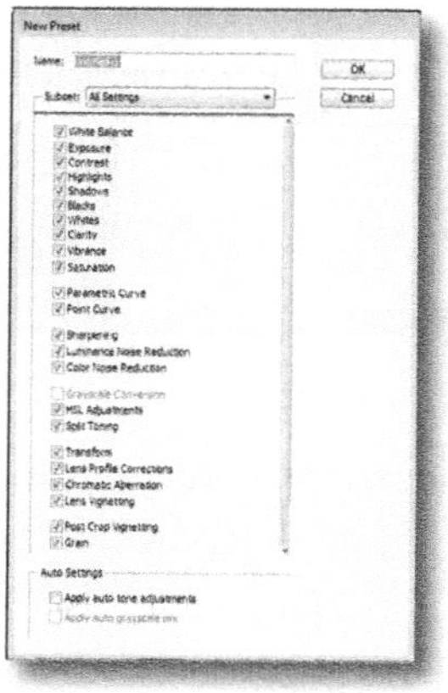

69 Tick any settings you want to save, give presct a name and click **OK**.

70 Back in Camera Raw click **Done** to close Camera Raw.

Now, back in Bridge, I'm going to show you how you can quickly and easily apply the preset you have created or remove it, without opening Camera Raw. Does it sound great? Of course, it does!

71 Back in Bridge, select any images that you want to apply a preset to.

72 Right-click on one of the images and choose **Develop Settings**:

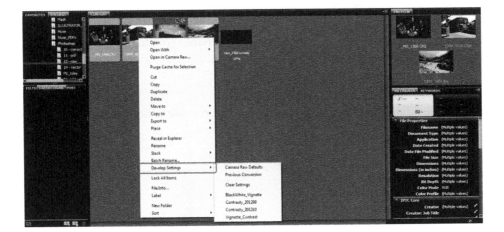

73 From the drop-down menu choose the name of the preset you have just created.

Bridge quickly applies your preset to all the images, even without you opening the images! This technique will save you so much precious time, trust me. And you can as easily apply the preset to three or four images as well as to a hundred images at the same time.

We're almost done. One more final step.

So, you've created a preset (or more) and you now know how to apply it to many images at the same time. What if you don't like the effect and want to remove it from the image? Well, that's easy as well. But first, let me show you how this all works. Where is all this information saved? Here's where. When you make adjustments to images in Camera Raw, all the changes are being saved to a sidecar file - a file with .XMP file extension. Let me show you that so that you can easily understand.

74 Using Explorer on Windows or Finder on Mac navigate to the folder with images you were editing in Camera Raw.

75 Next to each image you will see a sidecar file - the XMP file:

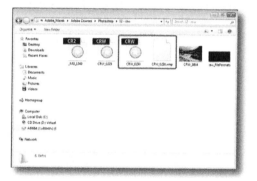

76 If you want to remove all the changes to the file, you can just delete the XMP file.

Or, there is another way of doing it in Adobe Bridge.

77 Navigate back to Bridge.

78 Select a file (or files) that you want to reverse back to its original look.

79 Right-click, choose **Develop Settings** and **Clear Settings**.

I thought I would finish with one more thing, maybe two, inside Adobe Camera Raw - something new in Camera Raw 8 inside Photoshop CC.

Radial Filter in Camera Raw 8 (Photoshop CC)

Camera Raw 8 is now part of Photoshop CC so I thought I would mention it here.

In Camera Raw 8, in Photoshop` CC, there is a new tool - **Radial Filter**:

Radial Filter in Camera Raw 8, in Photoshop CC, allows you to apply a number of adjustments as a circular mask.

Here are just some of the options that are available, when you select Radial filter:

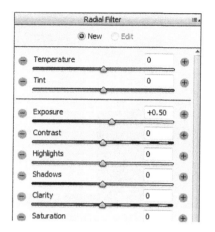

Here are the steps you can follow.

80 Open an image that you want to work with and select **Radial Filter** tool from the tools on the top of the Camera Raw.

81 On the right side of the interface choose the effect you want to apply.

82 Click and drag within the image to apply the effect.

Notice that the effect you are creating will appear outside the radial shape.

What I'm trying to do here is to darken the entire image except the front of the building:

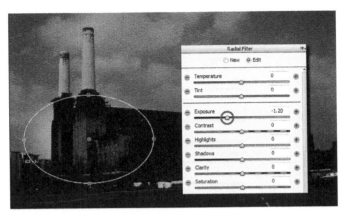

83 Let's take it to the next level. With the Radial Filter selected try adjusting Sharpness slider. Move it to the left to reduce sharpeness of the area around.

Here's what I've managed to create by lowering **Sharpeness**:

The area around the filter is out of focus! Very interesting effect and so easy to create.

There are a number of options here, so you could as easily desaturate a part of the image or increase the saturation of a part of the image as well. Once you've placed the filter on the image, you can drag the handles that appear to resize it or drag the circle in the centre of it to reposition it.

You can also add additional filters by clicking **New** button.

By default, when you apply the **Radial Filter**, the effect is being applied to the outside of the filter. However, you can also apply it to the area outside. Here's how:

84 Make sure you've applied the filter.

85 On the right side of Camera Raw, in options section, scroll down until you see **Effect**:

86 Next to Effect click **Inside** instead of Outside.

Ok, here's the new **Radial Filter** in a nutshell. I encourage you to keep experimenting and exploring all available features.

Now, let me show you one more great new feature inside Camera Raw 8 in Photoshop CC - **Spot Removal tool**.

Spot Removal in Camera Raw 8 (Photoshop CC)

Spot Removal is not a new feature in Camera Raw, you're right about that. However, something's changed in Spot Removal, something big. This will change the way you work with retouching images in Camera Raw, now in Photoshop CC.

87 Start by selecting **Spot Removal** tool:

In the past, Spot Removal tool was only available as a circle. But now, you can click and drag with the Spot Removal tool to create any shape and size you want for removing spots or unwanted objects on images.

88 Set the size for Spot Removal on the right side of Camera Raw.

89 Click and start dragging over the object you want to remove:

90 Release the mouse button and you will have a selection like nothing before:

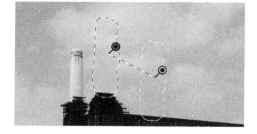

And the chimney is gone! That's the new Spot Removal tool in Photoshop CC!

Remember that Spot Removal tool in Camera Raw has two modes: **Heal** and **Clone** (a bit like Healing Brush and Clone Stamp in Photoshop):

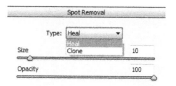

91 Close the image when done.

Note: Remember that anything you do inside Camera Raw is non-destructive and you can change it at any time.

Now turn the page over. I have a surprise for you...

This is kind of like a bonus chapter, but it's not a chapter. I thought I would share with you just one more great new feature in Photoshop CC.

This last feature inside Photoshop CC that I want to share with you is the ability to work with Camera Raw as a filter. Yes, Camera Raw is now available as a filter inside Photoshop CC. So, for example, if you start working on an image that is not a raw image so you can't open it in Camera Raw or maybe you are given a file with layers by a client, you can now do it as a filter in Photoshop CC.

Remember to convert a layer that you want to work on to a Smart Object and then apply Camera Raw as a filter like that:

1. *Select a layer,*

2. *Convert it to a Smart Object by right-clicking on a layer and selecting **Convert to Smart Object**,*

3. *Choose **Filter > Camera Raw Filter...***

This will open Camera Raw dialogue box where you will make adjustments to the image, and when you're done, just click OK to apply the settings and close the dialogue box.

Back to Photoshop, the layer will have Camera Raw filter applied to it, like that:

So now, whenever you want to change any of the settings in Camera Raw, you just double-click on the **Camera Raw Filter** below the layer in the Layers panel. This will open **Camera Raw** with all your settings remembered:

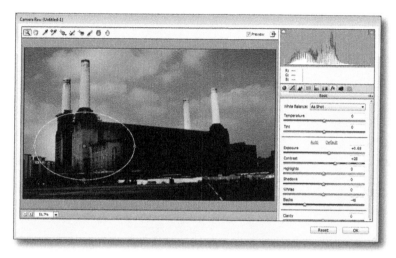

That's it! You're done!

You have finished your journey through the magical world of Adobe Photoshop CS6 / CC. Thank you for all the time we spent together and thank you for choosing me to be your guide.

405

Index

Lightning Source UK Ltd.
Milton Keynes UK
UKOW05f0658260815

257508UK00002B/20/P